Watchman Against the World

The Remarkable Journey

of Norman McLeod & his People

from Scotland to Cape Breton Island to New Zealand

Son of man, I have made thee a watchman unto the house of Israel: therefore hear the word at my mouth, and give them warning from me.

When I say unto the wicked, Thou shalt surely die; and thou givest him not warning, nor speakest to warn the wicked from his wicked way, to save his life; the same wicked man shall die in his iniquity; but his blood will I require at thine hand.

Yet if thou warn the wicked, and he turn not from his wickedness, nor from his wicked way, he shall die in his iniquity; but thou hast delivered thy soul.

Ezekiel iii. 17-19

Watchman Against the World

The Remarkable Journey *of* Norman McLeod & his People from Scotland to Cape Breton Island to New Zealand

by Flora McPherson

ILLUSTRATED

Breton Books
Wreck Cove, Cape Breton Island
1993

Design for Breton Books: Ronald Caplan
Production Assistance: Bonnie Thompson
Digital Scanning: Weldon Bona

ACKNOWLEDGEMENTS: For their permission to use the illustrations included in this book, thanks are due to the following:

The Alexander Turnbull Library for the prints of the ships *Gertrude*, *Spray*, *Breadalbane* and *Ellen Lewis*, from pencil drawings by John Alexander Munro, and for the photograph of Capt. Duncan McKenzie; J. D. Pascoe and the Alexander Turnbull Library for the photograph, "New Zealand coast looking towards Waipu"; E. Andrew and the General Assembly Library, Wellington, for the photograph of John Munro; Miss Ruth McDormand for "The Monument at St. Ann's"; New Brunswick Museum for the drawing of Norman McLeod from the Webster Collection; The Public Archives of Nova Scotia for "The handwriting of Norman McLeod"; J. B. White Ltd. for "The coast of Assynt in Scotland: Clachtoll Bay near Stoer." Oval photographs of Waipu pioneers are taken from *The Gael Fares Forth*; photographs of St. Ann's Harbour by Ronald Caplan originally appeared in *Cape Breton's Magazine*.

And thanks to Donald MacAulay, Baddeck, for providing prints of the 1903 photographs of the survivors of the emigration to New Zealand. And to W. James MacDonald of the St. Ann's-Baddeck/Waipu Twinning Society, who reminded us to include a map showing the remarkable voyage of Norman McLeod and his people.

Canadian Cataloguing in Publication Data
McPherson, Flora.
Watchman against the world

Previously published: London : R. Hale, 1962.
Includes bibliographical references.
ISBN 1-895415-20-9

1. McLeod, Norman, 1780-1866. 2. Presbyterians — Nova Scotia — Cape Breton Island — History — 19th century. 3. Presbyterians — New Zealand — History — 19th century. 4. Scots — Nova Scotia — Cape Breton Island — History — 19th century. 5. Scots — New Zealand — History — 19th century. 6. Scotland — Emigration and immigration — History — 19th century. I. Title.

EX9225.M258M32 1993 285'.2'092 C93-098552-4

Contents

Illustrations

Maps

Foreword

FACT AND LEGEND meet and blend and sometimes clash in the story of Norman McLeod. To write of him and his people is to make many choices among the tales which have passed down orally through the generations, and to reconcile them with the fragments of recorded fact. I hope that unwitting errors in choice of detail may be redeemed by the total picture of the man, his times and his relationship to his community.

In my search for a true impression I am indebted to many libraries. They vary in size from the Library of Congress to the charming little library in the village of Caledonia, New York. They range in location from the library of the University of Western Ontario in my home city of London to the Alexander Turnbull Library in Wellington, New Zealand. Between these extremes are many other helpful libraries, notably the library of Knox College, Toronto, the Legislative Library of Nova Scotia and the Archives of the United Church of Canada. From all I have received generous and efficient assistance.

Special thanks go to the staff of the Public Archives of Nova Scotia who not only provide a minutely catalogued collection of valuable materials but also by their sympathy and enthusiasm make every research project their own.

I am grateful to these custodians of history and also to its original recorders—to Judge Patterson for his manuscript history and his historical notes, to all the people in Cape Breton communities who recognized important events and took time to write of them, and to the people like Mrs. Kathryn MacKenzie of Baddeck who did not write, but cherished the past in their minds and brought it forth fresh and exciting.

My greatest debt, however, is to several New Zealand writers who, as well as the opportunity of knowing the early settlers of Waipu and their descendants, had the interest and skill to preserve their story. N. R. McKenzie in *The Gael Fares Forth* and Neil Robinson in *Lion of Scotland* record countless details no longer available elsewhere. I hope that in some small measure this retelling of the Canadian segment of the story may complement their careful research.

Finally my thanks to everyone who has tolerated or assisted my writing; above all, to my friend Mary Barber who advised and criticized, read and re-read, and kept believing in this book.

Flora McPherson

CHAPTER ONE

A Child of Assynt

FROM THE HIGHLANDS of Cape Breton the Cabot Trail winds down the rocky coast toward the quiet waters of the Bras d'Or Lake. Beside the road, against the gentle hills and the bay of St. Ann's, stands a granite millstone. It is inscribed:

> Rev. Norman McLeod
> 1780-1866
>
> As clergyman, schoolmaster and magistrate he moulded the character of this community for a generation. Born at Stoer Point, Assynt, Scotland, he emigrated to Pictou in 1817, led his band of Scots to St. Ann's in 1820 and remained here until 1851, when he again led his followers first to Australia and finally to New Zealand.

In the village of Waipu, New Zealand, is a tall pillar. A defiant lion stands on its summit. Carved on the six sides of its base are sailing ships—the *Margaret*, the *Highland Lass*, the *Gertrude*, the *Spray*, the *Breadalbane*, the *Ellen Lewis*. It is the monument for pioneers—eight hundred people and the ships that brought them halfway around the world with Norman McLeod.

The stern coastline of northwestern Scotland is broken by fierce thrusts of the sea. It is an empty land. Only a few scattered crofts mark the jagged promontory of Stoer Point. It has no monument, but it is there that the story begins.

When, in the last years of the eighteenth century, a man of the northern Highlands looked beyond himself for security, he had two resources—his God and his tribe.

In the world around him there was little comfort. Bare mountains towered over his rugged land. At their bases and in the country by the Atlantic shore the gloomy heath was studded with piles of grey rocks. Worn into weird shapes, they stood eerie in the twilight or the half-light of an approaching storm. Not even a light ribbon of road cut the brooding blackness of the land.

The sounds, too, were harsh and austere. Breakers crashed on the western shore. Inland the sounds were of water dashing down the hillsides, of rain lashed by endless days of western wind, and of the birds' wild cries.

A man could not face such a land alone. From the earliest times he had made it tractable by peopling it with spirits whom he could address and propitiate. Still in the last days of the eighteenth century the mountaintops glowed with Beltane fires on the first of May. Through them all the cattle of the country were driven so that they would be safe until the next May Day. Water-kelpies roared in swollen streams and fairies flitted among the spindly birches. Traditional rites preserved the crops and libations of milk were poured out to the spirits of the farmyard.

For some Highlanders the Christian religion was only another protection against ill fate. To them there was nothing incongruous in praying to the Christian God to preserve their wives and their children, their sheep and their cattle, from the power and dominion of the fairies, and from the malicious effects of every evil eye. To live free of these familiar fears and be strong enough to stand against their overwhelming land, they needed a powerful God, not a God of love, but a being with the stern austerity of the tribal Jehovah.

To the Highlanders as to the ancient Israelites the tribe was long the human symbol of security. They did not need the possession of land or the stable organization of a town, but only a body of people to which they could belong. While their security was in the tribe they were free to lead a nomadic life without attachment to place or possessions. Long before the eighteenth century, each tribe or clan had assumed certain areas of land as its own, but still their chief's power lay not in his right as a landlord but in his lineal descent from the old patriarchs. His power was unchanged even if he lost his estates.

To his followers he parcelled out land as they required it, but each man's holdings were impermanent, and could be changed to meet the needs of other members of the clan. In their chief was the ultimate authority, their protection against poverty and want, their defence against all outside forces, even against just punishment for their crimes. In return they owed him labour and service and absolute loyalty.

By the latter half of the eighteenth century there was peace in the Highlands. Men no longer needed the physical protection of the clan, nor did their chief require them to defend his honour or his lands. At the same time, social and economic progress were gradually transferring to other agencies the old economic functions of the clan. The chief as landlord was replacing the chief as leader. When safety no longer demanded that the chief's men should be clustered around him, he was free to make other uses of his vast mountainous lands. Often they were turned into sheep farms. The crofters' little hillside plots were in the way. There were evictions, misunderstandings, and bitterness against the landlord.

The tribal organization was weakening but the tribal tradition remained. There was still a place in the people's lives for a leader who belonged to them, to be the centre of the tribal unity which existed although its outward forms and practices were gone. There were temporary local heroes, exalted by feats of physical strength or daring, but the man to whom the Highlander would give his loyalty had to be more than these. He had to be a man of mental, physical and spiritual strength, of courage, of daring imagination—he had to be, in himself, greater than any hereditary chief, to claim and hold in his own right the place that was empty at the heart of the tribe.

Such a place awaited Norman McLeod. He was born in 1780, near Stoer Point, one of the rocky promontories jutting from the western coast of Scotland into the treacherous waters of the North Minch. In distant lands, unheard of by the little neighbourhood that celebrated his birth that September day, Norman would try, through the eighty-six years of his life, to determine and to meet the need of his people. Wherever he lived, his conception of his role as their leader would be shaped by his first thirty years in his home parish in the Scottish Highlands.

The parish was called Assynt, a Gaelic word meaning "in

and out," a symbol both of the coastline and of the jagged mountainous surface. With one arable acre in every hundred acres of land, Assynt was the most rugged part of the rugged county of Sutherland. Among its rocks and mountains the people made their living.

Their homes crouched together in the valleys or straggled along the Atlantic shore. One of the coastal cottages was the home of Norman's parents, Daniel and Margaret McLeod. Its walls were of alternate layers of stone and turf; birch timbers, bent into a semicircle and covered with thin sods, formed the roof. Through a hole drifted the smoke from the peat fire. The hearth was the centre of the room below. On a good day, there was also light from holes in the roof at the top of the walls. When the winds were strong, or the west wind brought long days of rain, the holes could be plugged with a sod or a bunch of straw. Then the room was lighted only by the dull glow of the fire, or by the burning brands of bog-fir whose fantastic shapes cast weird shadows on the walls.

It was the usual home of the north Highland tenants. So for centuries they had existed within a land that they could not hope to change. To their minister, William Mackenzie, their patient endurance of hunger, cold and fatigue was worthy of praise, but enforced patience could easily become a habit and decline into torpid acceptance. Since, by the old run-rig system of tillage a different part of the common land was assigned to each farmer annually, there had been no incentive to make improvements, no reward for initiative. Although by 1780 the system had been abolished and the tenants granted long leases, they had no tradition of progress to spur them toward accomplishment.

Neither was there an incentive to self-improvement in the personal pride which the clan system had nourished, with each man's security not in his possessions or accomplishments but in his name alone. It was early in the century that Defoe saw in Edinburgh "a man in his mountain habit, armed with a broadsword, a target, a pistol, at his girdle a dagger, and staff, walking down the High Street as upright and haughty as if he were a lord, and withal driving a cow." The law now prohibited bearing arms but the lordly mien was unchanged. For what, beyond his minimum physical needs, would such a man work?

Hopeless of progress or proudly indifferent to it, each new generation followed its parents' ways. Soon change would come, but in 1780, life along the western shore moved in its age-old pattern.

It was harvest time when Norman was born. The barley crop was good, and the men were content as they cut the grain by hand and carried it to the tiny stone barns that dotted the rocky shore. This year it might see them through till spring.

No sooner was the barley safely housed than the potatoes had to be dug, placed in pits and thoroughly covered with turf against the approaching winter, for although the snow was seldom heavy on the shores of Assynt, the frosts were hard. With the harvest over, the young cattle, sturdy little black beasts which were the staple of the parish, were taken to the winterings, nearby hill-sides preserved during harvest months to be used now for winter pasture. Probably a few days after Norman's birth his mother was again milking the cows which had been left to feed beside her door, or to take shelter in the byre at the end of the house.

The scanty milk of the poor straw-fed cows, potatoes boiled in sea-water because there was no salt, and thin cakes of barley bread sustained the family through the long northern winter. The McLeods, like other coastal people, got herring from the shore fisheries. So they lived and waited for spring.

When February came, it was time to take their crooks and gather in the seaweed which the winter storms had driven on to the shore. They piled it into creels hung on the horses' backs and spread it over the fields as fertilizer. At the end of the month they began to plough their rocky fields without horses or oxen, using a home-made implement which they called the *cas chrom* (crooked leg). This tool was shaped like a hockey stick, with a piece of wood projecting sideways at the junction of the shaft and the iron-sheathed blade. The projection served as a step for the user's foot to push the implement diagonally into the soil. Then, with a jerk on the upper end of the handle, he turned the soil over.

After delving, the ground was left until the end of April

when it was harrowed by hand with a wooden harrow. Then it was ploughed a second time and barley was sown. At about the same time, potatoes were planted, and sometimes a little patch of cabbages beside the cottage.

In April, too, when the grass was growing again, came the "lifting." The young cattle were taken to join the sheep, goats and horses in the rocky pasture of the upper hillsides. The ceremony was well named, for the poor beasts could barely stand, weak from months of starving on the sparse winterings and in the filthy darkness of the byre. For the summer, in the outer pasture beyond the hillside dykes, the livestock of all the tenant farmers fed in common.

Now the cycle of survival had begun once more. In June the peats were cut. At the end of the month, the cows, which had been feeding on the green grass near the buildings, were driven up to the shieling or hill pastures where they were kept for the summer. The whole household moved with them and settled in a little stone hut on the mountainside. There they lived happily on milk and cheese and the wild berries which they picked on the hills. Since the cows were women's work, the men could spend the summer working for the herring busses, the vessels which came every year to their shores.

Farming was the basic industry of the parish and set the pattern of its life. Fishing was the supplement which gave the coastal people hope of more than bare subsistence, even of a small profit. In his report of the parish, William Mackenzie explained, "Properly speaking, there are no seamen here; but if tugging an oar in a boisterous sea can be called the accomplishment of seamen, all the tenants along the coast are seamen."[1] Each of the coastal farms had one or more boats which fished in summer for the herring fleet.

The fishermen were sure of a market. In a good herring season as many as eighty ships from every part of the Scottish coast would come to the large harbour of Loch Inver. These herring busses rode at anchor in the harbour, and each morning the little boats clustered around them, waiting their turn to unload the night's catch.

[1] Sinclair, John, *Statistical Account of Scotland*, v. 16, p. 198.

For a man with the alert mind of Daniel McLeod, the annual coming of the fishing fleet did more than promise that a few pounds might be left in his pocket after his rent was paid. Through the fleet he touched the world outside. He talked with fishermen who in their home ports had known sailors from around the world, who themselves had seen far-off places. Unlike his neighbours, Daniel could understand them all, since he spoke both Gaelic and English. From his fishing, Daniel had money to spend. He bought books. To his mind, challenged by the problems of faith and religion which were exciting Scotland, books opened another door upon the world. Richard Baxter, Philip Doddridge, John Bunyan, learned Episcopalians like Bishop Hall, Archbishop Tillotson, and Judge Hale—all manner of distinguished scholars and controversialists came in his books to the cottage of Daniel McLeod.

Margaret McLeod was unabashed in their presence. Although toward Daniel she preserved the decorous respect required of a wife, she was a woman of keen and independent mind. She had been a member of the Church of England, and, for reasons of conscience, had left it to become an Independent. Such a step was not taken lightly. In a community whose thinkers had nothing but religious doctrine to challenge their minds, her action would be scrutinized and questioned. Margaret was ready to meet all her adversaries—even her husband who belonged to the Established Church of Scotland.

What was there for a child in such a world? Within its limits it was secure. The pattern was unchanged from year to year: in the spring there was ploughing and sowing and the cutting of the peats; in the summer the light-hearted freedom of the shieling; in autumn the harvest; in winter the gathering from the darkness into the circle of the fire.

A child would know the dangers, too. From the cottage door he could watch the little boats fighting their way toward the harbour. He knew the stories of those that had struck the jagged rocks. He knew the rivulets that in the sunshine sparkled gently down the hills, and in a day of rain became tremendous torrents. Old women told of travellers lured to their death at the fords.

They told other tales: wistful stories of Fingal and the Celtic heroes of long ago; stories of later times, of Macleods, Mackays and Mackenzies, their feuds and their mighty deeds. There were songs, too—mysteriously sad, to make a little child stand close against his mother, or send a boy away into the darkened world beyond the firelight; gay and daring, to brighten dreamy eyes and set the children dancing.

When it was time, Norman took the path to the head of Loch Assynt. There, at the foot of craggy Glasven, beside the familiar church, was the newly-built parish school. It was a sturdy stone building with glass windows and a neatly thatched roof. To Norman's family the learning which it represented was all important. Precocious, keen to learn and to excel, Norman eagerly entered the school and the new surroundings.

After school the pupils could explore the castle. Near the school, on the lake shore it stood, empty and grey. It alone of the parish buildings had stairs, though the steps were crumbling, and at the top of the fourth flight one could look through the narrow window-slit, far down the loch into the west, proudly, as Donald McLeod must have looked when he built the castle two hundred years before. Norman was not of the blood of the chief, although as a clansman he bore the name, but he had seen the McLeod from Ross-shire who was of the chief's family. Though the man looked like any man, Norman saw an old lady take his hand and vow that she would never give to any other the hand that had been touched by a descendant of her chief

The castle had long been empty. Storms were wearing it down, but it still stood, symbol of inspiration, conflict, and authority in the old Highlands. Beside it, sound and firm, stood the church which was to inspire, divide, and rule the new.

CHAPTER TWO

The Problem of Irreverence

THE ROSY FACE and cheery round figure of William Mackenzie had long represented the church in the parish of Assynt. He had come, young and newly licensed, under the patronage of the Earl of Sutherland, in 1765. He was to remain until his death, more than fifty years later.

To his people, the minister stood for everything beyond their daily struggle for existence; he also represented them to the outside world. He was the one man who could know them in all aspects of their life; on him the government depended for its official information about his parish. Parson William, in his reports, shows only a perfunctory interest in his people. He cites as his accomplishment the introduction of the cultivation of the potato in 1766, but from that time he seems to have made little contribution of any kind, and is so disinterested that after thirty years of tenure he is still making excuses for his lack of information. His people are landscape figures whom he observes with condescending approval; their "noble lord" he salutes with fulsome compliments.

He is portrayed not only by his own words but also by John Kennedy whose father became Mackenzie's missionary assistant: "Mr. William Mackenzie was almost all a minister ought not to be, yet he continued to occupy his charge until his death. Always accustomed to regard his pastoral work as an unpleasant condition of drawing his stipend, he reduced it to the smallest possible dimensions and would not infrequently be absent without reason and without leave for many weeks from his charge. This was the usual practice in these days of the moderate stipend-lifters of Sutherland. The visit of one of them to Ross-shire would be an affair of a month's length, at the least, and the people never clamoured for his return. The beadle who was also the parson's gillie, invariably accompanied the minister on these excursions. In one case the beadle was also the piper of the district and during his absence with the minister on one of his jaunts, a parishioner was asked when he expected the minister to return. 'I don't know and I don't care,' was his reply, 'if he had only left the piper he might stop away as long as he wished.'

"During the latter part of his life, 'Parson William' was much addicted to drink. This was known to Presbytery but could not easily be proved. The people were unwilling to complain and to give evidence against him. The awe of his office was on them in spite of all the irregularity of his life, and as a man and a neighbour he was rather a favourite."[1]

It is almost impossible to overestimate the importance of the minister in the life of an eighteenth-century Scottish parish. He was not merely, among many officials, the one whose particular concern was spiritual guidance. Other than the laird and his factor, he was the one official the people knew. The church which hc represented controlled education in the parish schools. For all but criminal offences its elders controlled, rebuked and punished the parishioners. It was responsible for the poor. In Assynt they received an annual income of 2s. 2d. "There are a few pounds collected annually for fines for anti-nuptial delinquency," Mackenzie reported. "The annual session censure is commuted for the payment of one or two pounds for the poor of the parish." Since his people were unusually well-behaved, the poor generally had to be supported by their relatives.

Not only the range of his authority but his salary established the pre-eminence of the minister. In Assynt domestic servants were paid one pound sterling per annum with food and clothing provided. Day labourers, highly paid because of the high wages of the fishing fleet, got 10d. per day with three meals. For fish packing, skilful men got 2s. a day, and "strong old women and lasses got 1s. 6d. per day gutting herrings." The parish school master, in 1794, got £8 6s. 8d., probably supplemented by students' fees. In that same year, the minister received 87 pounds. It is no wonder that he was considered a person set apart.

[1] Kennedy, John, *The Days of the Fathers in Ross-shire*, p. 190.

In the Highlands, too, the minister had a people already submissive to unseen forces. The supernatural and the mysterious had long been familiar. In their stern land, human disaster and death were touched by the majestic austerity of tragedy. The readiness for such moments was always with them; they met disaster with sombre satisfaction, almost with relief. The God into whose hands they fell was stern and just; with awe they regarded his representative. Norman McLeod recalled that as a little boy he thought that the most pious of men must be those employed about the dead—the grave-diggers and coffin-makers. In another sphere, beyond comparison with common men, he placed the ministers of his church.

The most exciting events of the year were also of the Church. These were the Communion seasons, the occasions on which the sacrament of the Lord's Supper was administered. From June to August a number of parishes combined to hold communion, each in turn. The parishes of Sutherland, including Assynt, each had communion only once in two years to save the expense of the elements which cost three pounds. When the occasion came it was solemn, festive and memorable.

On Thursday, the fast day, the people began to arrive. From as many as forty parishes they came, whole families, carrying the food they needed and the woollen plaids that would keep them warm for the nights in the neighbourhood houses and barns or on the open hillsides. Ministers came too, from the neighbouring parishes. To the crowds on the hills they preached in Gaelic; for the English congregation there was a service that day in the church.

Friday was the day of self-examination. In the summer sunshine, or, with equal patience, in a chilling drizzle, the people heard long hours of testimony and disputation. The only shelter was the "tent" for the ministers. Oars were set up on end to form a cone, blankets were draped over them, and in front was fixed a board on which the Bible was placed. From the tent the ministers looked up at the hillsides—the black and white shepherds' plaids, the soft blues and greys of the other homespun fabrics, splashes of tartan, no longer forbidden, brilliant against the slopes.

All the visitors tried to arrive for the Friday meeting, for this was the day when someone from their home parish might be called to "speak to the question"—a text was proposed, and its meaning expounded by one or more of the ministers; then the parish minister called by name on an outstanding layman from a visiting parish to speak about the subject from his own interpretation and experience. From the hillside would arise a grotesque figure. A black cloak trailed to his heels and a knotted handkerchief, once white, perched like a shrunken dustcap on his long greasy hair. His Gaelic speech was soft at first, almost hesitant; as he spoke it rose, stronger, more certain, till it was pouring out in a passionate torrent. His cloak tossed, his hair flapped against his shoulders. This was one of "the men."

"The men" were so called because, though not ministers, they were set apart. In their own parishes they had first been singled out by their ministers who marked them as unusually devout and profoundly gripped by spiritual problems. They were asked first to pray and then to "speak to the question" at the meetings of their own congregation. Gradually, a man so chosen separated himself from the ordinary doings of men. Like an Old Testament prophet, he often spent a night alone in the hills in meditation and prayer. Then he would sweep down into the valley with a new revelation of the Spirit or a message of doom for the wayward or the purveyors of false doctrines.

Any ministers who, in their sight, were ungodly, "the men" publicly condemned. Although the ministers might, in their turn, abuse "the men" in the Church courts, they could not shake their hold on the people who believed them divinely inspired. For a time they were heroes to young Norman. He thought that "no men on earth had closer communion with heaven" and that there could be "no higher religious attainment" than to be one of them. When time had changed his view, his scorn was as great as his admiration once had been. Many years later he described them: "It would be almost equal for you in my native country to object to the good sense and piety of St. Peter or St. Paul as to the superior wisdom and spirituality of the men in question! These spiritual men will not take a single text of the Bible in its literal sense or meaning, for that would be only legality and like legal preachers who have not the 'Spirit.' To mystify and spiritualize the plainest literal and historical facts must be the province of these semi-supernatural beings."[2]

Perhaps thirty men would "speak to the question" on the Communion Friday. Then, the long day's discussion ended, the weary people straggled away for the night. Saturday was the day of preparation with the ministers preaching to the crowds, and with prayer meetings throughout the parish in the evening. Finally the Sabbath with its admonitions to new professors, warnings to unworthy receivers, and the great goblet passing up and down the long wooden tables.

On Monday, the day of thanksgiving, they gathered once more before the long journey home. For some this season was the renewal of faith which would sustain them through the hardship and futility of the coming year. Some found in it only a vague inspiration, some an intellectual stimulus, others a happy reunion with scattered relatives and friends. They prayed, they gossiped, they made love, they caroused; though the purpose was holy the people were human still. Sometimes they were very tired of looking inward and straining upward.

The minister was pre-eminent in the government of the Scottish Church, but in the Presbyterian system he was not an uncontrolled dictator. The tradition of his selection by the vote of the church members implied that he was their servant as well as their leader. It was a blow at the very roots of this democratic system when, early in the eighteenth century, an Act of the British Parliament gave the patronage of church livings to the county lairds. Henceforth, by their appointment rather than by popular vote the minister was to be selected.

Immediately there were protests, not only against the denial of the individual's right of selection, but against the implied subjection of Church to State. Groups broke away from the Established Church even though the price of their rebellion was loss of State support. They formed congregations of dissenters, and frequently, since rebellion had produced them, rebellion separated them. They divided within themselves and seceded from one another.

[2] McLeod, Norman, *The Present Church of Scotland and a Tint of Normanism Contending in a Dialogue*, p. 254.

The original issue was the principle of patronage. As time went on, the greater protest was against the ministers, liberal to the point of laxity and indifference, whom some patrons had appointed. The people, taught to read in the new parish schools, were poring over their principal book, the Bible. To it the Highlanders turned their intellectual hunger and their mystical imagination, but they found little response to the growing intensity of their individual religious experience in the worldly liberality of many of their clergy. Devout earnest men cried out against the ministers. Men with high motives, sometimes with narrow passionate minds, pleaded for a deeper faith and a firmer doctrine. Many of their leaders were great preachers whose piety and intensity would give new fire to the Church; the same qualities in lesser men became fanaticism and a stifling bigotry.

Despite the rising tumult in the Church, the parish of Assynt, at the end of the century, was still drifting along in outward conformity. Norman finished school and took his place with the other young men of the parish in the routine of fishing and farming. There his vigorous strength made him a leader, but he was not satisfied. His mind was eager, too. He devoured every book he could find, at home or anywhere within his reach. They had but one theme—theology.

As an old man he described the years of his lonely search. First, he said, his reading and curiosity led him into Roman Catholicism and he was for a certain period a Papist. When he "got disentangled from that delusion" he next fell into Universalism. "I was taken in that snare for about a year and a half; which, after sucking very plausible doctrines indeed, I found as destructive as my former deception.... Heaven knows what mental suffering these things cost me! After that Infidelity, or in other words both Deism and Atheism arrested and infested my very soul, for at least two whole years; but not so much, like my other errors, from the reading of wicked or infidel books as by deistical and atheistical suggestions, piercing my very spirit.... Quakery affected my mind, rather unknown, at the time, to any but myself. For some time, however, I relinquished secret devotion, not from any disregard to religion or its serious concerns, but from Quakerly sentiments, fearing it more offensive to Heaven to perform any devotional duties without what I esteemed the presence...of the Holy Spirit, than a suspension of my external worship. This brought on me a lingering decay in the inward man, till I was drawn into the gulf of temptation....

"My next trial and temptation fell out on the ground of Arminianism. I read much on that subject and indulged my family to do the same, probably too far. But under a long and heavy fever, and in my great weakness of body and mind; and under the deep desertion of my wonted spiritual peace and joy, for the space of six weeks, I believed—or at least fearfully dreaded—I was fallen from grace. This was by far the heaviest affliction that has ever arrested my soul."[3]

The faith which at last he found remained secure. He fully accepted the doctrine of Calvin, and the tremendous responsibility of being one of God's elect.

Norman had won through to this conviction when, in 1806, the Society for Promoting Christian Knowledge sent Rev. John Kennedy as a missionary assistant to the parish minister. At first sight the people were attracted to him. He was thirty-five years old, tall, fair, phenomenally strong, with a step so light it barely bent the heather. As they knew him they found that his scholarship was not remarkable but that he made no pretensions to great knowledge. His speech had no tricks of manner or style. He was a sincere, unassuming, devout man who was deeply concerned for them and whom they came to love.

There could have been no greater contrast to William Mackenzie, even in worldly matters. Mackenzie thriftily farmed his glebe and had built a little mill to grind his grain and save the cost of a servant; Kennedy was so unworldly that of all the animals about the manse his favourite pony was the only one which he could ever recognize as his own. Their difference in spiritual things was even greater. Fortunately, Mackenzie was sufficiently indifferent to give Kennedy a free hand. They met as little as possible. Kennedy consulted him only when absolutely necessary, carried on the parish work in his own way and was rarely interfered with.

As he looked over his new congregation, John Kennedy

[3] ibid., p. 248.

would mark at once the young man whose black head towered so proudly above them. Norman, like him, was famous for his strength. They must have felt the sudden mutual attraction of physical champions. But the fierce grey eyes which probed and questioned Kennedy's words were in a harder face than his, and they flashed with a proud, undisciplined spirit. Kennedy's missionary zeal was challenged by this haughty young man of whom he had been warned as a "clever, irreverent, forward youth."

The problem of irreverence was gone. Norman had won through to a firm religious conviction. Into it he turned all the keenness of his mind and the intensity of his spirit. He "at once started in the course of profession, at a stature and with a courage that seemed never to have known a childhood at all."[4] Probably Norman's highest aim was still to be one of "the men."

It was natural that Kennedy should try to guide and restrain him. With gentle thoroughness he hoped to lead him gradually into understanding and participation. Norman had fought the problem through by himself, he had made his decision alone, he would brook no opposition. Kennedy's son says that the conflict with Norman was the greatest trial of his father's life. Norman, in later times, spoke respectfully of Kennedy. Very probably it was the challenge of John Kennedy which turned Norman from mystical spirituality to sound scholarship, and sent him from the farm and fishery to the college at Aberdeen.

[4] Kennedy, op. cit., p. 193.

CHAPTER THREE

The Making of a Rebel

SEVEN YEARS of preparation stood between Norman and the ministry—a long delay for an impatient man already twenty-seven years old. He could accept it only in his conviction of the great mission to which he was called, and in the security of the spiritual authority which he was already beginning to hold in his community.

Nor for him only would the time be long. Mary McLeod, who was in love with Norman, had expected, like every other girl in the parish, to be married by the time she was twenty-one. Gently she had tried to support him through his doubts and confusion, she had endured his black silences, she had waited and feared when his surges of recklessness carried him and his tiny fishing boat into the wildest seas. Now his faith and his goal were sure, the people were seeing his transformation as a miracle, turning to him as an authority. For Mary it should be an honour, not a shame to wait for him, to share in small measure the setting apart which already removed Norman from the rest. But while she gloried in his triumph, she must often have wondered what would be her place in the life of the confident Norman who set out that October day for Aberdeen.

His long walk, over one hundred and fifty miles of moor and mountain and rough new road, brought him for the first time to people who were organized and busy. Nearly 30,000 of them there were, living, working, planning a prosperous future in the bustling port of Aberdeen. Ships from many lands were in the harbour. Dutch and German voices bellowed their orders as their cargoes swung aboard. Scots shouted through the beat of the carpenters' hammers in the shipyards by the shore. The shipyards were going at full speed for these were the years when Aberdeen was building more ships than any other port in

Scotland. There were rich new opportunities in the American trade, and as the great war with Napoleon went on, more and more ships were needed near home. Men flocked to Aberdeen to learn the shipbuilders' skills.

Norman would notice the harbour first. Soon he would also know of the thriving textile industries, the breweries, brick works, nail factories, the paper factories which answered the local need for books and newspapers, the iron foundries which were filling the new demand for agricultural implements in the Highlands. No doubt he looked with professional interest at the busy fish market at the foot of the Shiprow and examined the paving stones which the new granite industry was shipping to London.

Aberdeen was well launched into Scotland's new era. It showed its prosperity in its solid institutions—grammar schools, infirmary, hospitals and charity schools, the record office, the Aberdeen bank. As Norman walked through the narrow streets, the Aberdonians would expect him to admire their newest buildings—the theatre on Marischal Street, the Custom House on the quay, the military barracks on Castle Hill, and the lunatic asylum northwest of the town.

Not only in the structure of its buildings but of its society Aberdeen belonged to a different world from Norman's home parish. It was full of organizations. There were benevolent societies, religious tract societies, friendly societies—the masonic lodges and the associations of ship masters, dyers, porters—the Sabbath evening school society, the education societies. The poor were supported by the United Fund, formed by the junction of several funds previously under separate management, raising money from annual subscription.

The local newspaper was weekly, but in the Athenaeum reading room, for the annual subscription of one guinea and a half, there were available all the "respectable newspapers" and many of the periodical works published in London and Edinburgh, also maps, sea charts and atlases. There were also several circulating libraries and congregational libraries.

Not all of these benefits would be available to Norman as he strode along the street in his scarlet college gown. He had too little money for some pleasures; others would be barred by the intensity of his purpose. But the atmosphere of the city would touch him; its organization would appeal to his incisive mind. He must have observed even if he did not take part. When he got up from his books a man who loved the sea would turn to the harbour to watch the clean sharp lines of the ships taking shape in the builders' hands.

It was two miles from the quay to King's College in the High Street of Old Aberdeen, but he could see the stone lantern and crown which surmounted its square tower standing above the squat grey buildings of the town. It was a proud college, one of the oldest in Scotland, founded in 1494. Among the buildings surrounding its quadrangular court, the most significant was the library. It was the library which attracted prospective ministers and teachers to King's in preference to the plain centrally-situated Marischal College whose new observatory proclaimed its scientific interests. King's library was fortunate both in its rare old manuscripts and in its complete contemporary collection, its variety assured, since the college had a right to a copy of every book entered in Stationers' Hall—a gold mine for Norman with his deep unsatisfied need for books.

The college session began on the first Monday of November and ended on the last Friday of March. In the seven free months there was ample time for a strong, experienced man like Norman to earn the cost of a winter's study. Tuition fees were not exorbitant (twenty guineas for the entire four-year arts course), and, like most of the students, he could exist for the winter in the cheapest available lodgings. There he studied Greek, mathematics, natural history, natural philosophy and moral philosophy which made up the arts course. With a gold medal in moral philosophy, Norman graduated in 1812.[1]

To Norman, intent on his future ministry, the city's churches would be as important as his college. He could find them of

[1] Although the fact of Norman's graduation is not corroborated by the present records of the University of Aberdeen, legend and tradition give it abundant support. In his letters he addressed as old college friends men who are recorded as graduates of King's College. The people of his settlement, many of whom had known him in his youth, accepted him as a graduate of the college, and one of his New Zealand biographers reports that Mary is known to have worn as an ornament the medal which he won.

every kind in Aberdeen. Probably because they were a busy prosperous people whose minds were stimulated by many subjects other than theology, the Aberdonians had a long tradition of hospitality to all types of faith. In the centuries of their persecution, Roman Catholics had found a haven in Aberdeen. They were even allowed to buy land in the name of a Protestant friend and to build a chapel on it. In the Church of Scotland, too, when episcopacy was first abolished, the Aberdonians had gone their own way and kept their bishop for years.

Now they had all kinds of Presbyterians. In the three decades before Norman came to Aberdeen, fifteen new churches and chapels were built, nine of them for nine different dissenting groups. They had come from protests against patronage, and from demands for reform in the practices of the Church and in the relation of Church and State. For the first time Norman met dissenters not as rebel individuals, but as organized rebel groups. Each summer when he returned to work in Assynt he continued his own rivalry with John Kennedy. He found more and more people who would follow him, he knew the heady feeling of capturing men's imaginations. Now he could feel not only his power over them as their leader, but the potential power of the group under his leadership.

With the security promised by his arts degree and with the earnings of his long summers as a temporary income Norman married Mary McLeod. In their country of many McLeods their identical surnames did not necessarily denote a family relationship. Mary, now twenty-five years old, had never altered in her devotion to Norman, nor in her thoughtful preparation for the role which would be hers in three years when he had completed his course in divinity. But for the present she remained at home in Assynt while Norman went to Edinburgh to continue his studies.

The Edinburgh to which he came was a very different place from the busy commercial city of Aberdeen. This city of about 75,000 people was entering the brilliant period which was to be known as her Augustan Age. In the later years of the eighteenth century the city had broken away from the huddle of wynds and closes which formed the Old Town, and had crossed the

Nor'Loch to build the spacious and elegant New Town. It had known a great period of literary and philosophical distinction—David Hume, Adam Smith, Tobias Smollett, Principal William Robertson of the university, had distinguished it in the eighteenth century, and Robert Burns had been a momentary plaything of its social world. To it in the early nineteenth century came the massive intellect of Thomas Carlyle. These were the years when it was to be romanticized to the world and to itself by the genius of Sir Walter Scott.

It was a place where literary and cultural values were no longer challenged. The General Assembly of the Church, which had rated its ministers for attending the theatrical performance of Douglas a few decades before, now altered the times of its meetings so that they would not be depleted by the rival attraction of Mrs. Siddons at the Theatre Royal. To the impoverished students the literary pleasures of the city were not available, but they could sense its atmosphere. They lodged, not at the college, but in the City. Although they might live in miserable hovels and pore diligently over their books, they touched, even on the streets, the life of Edinburgh.

Thomas Carlyle, who was also a student at the university in those years, recalled the world he saw on Princes Street on a sunny afternoon. "All that was brightest in Edinburgh seemed to have stept out to enjoy, in the fresh pure air, the finest city-prospect in the world and the sight of one another, and was gaily streaming this way and that. The crowd was lively enough, brilliant, many-coloured, many-voiced, clever-looking (beautiful and graceful womankind a conspicuous element); crowd altogether elegant, polite, and at its ease tho' on parade; something as if of unconsciously rhythmic in the movement of it, as if of harmonious in the sound of its cheerful voices, bass and treble, fringed with light laughter: a quite pretty kind of natural concert and rhythmus of march; into which, if at leisure, and carefully enough dressed (as some of us seldom were) you might introduce yourself and flow for a turn or two with the general flood."[2]

[2] Carlyle, Thomas, "Christopher North," *The Nineteenth Century*, v. 87, p. 104, January 1920.

How Norman would stalk through that worldly assembly! To him this city would be far more alien than Aberdeen. Aberdeen's practical commercialism he could understand, and within its limits, accept. This social assurance and liberal worldliness, possible only to a people which has not known the struggle for survival, were to him deeply suspect. Most profoundly disturbing was the reflection of this spirit in the ministers of his church whom he had once so greatly revered. It seemed that for many of them the principal concern was to be men of the world, presentable in society; only incidentally were they interested in their spiritual calling. Norman, whose faith was a passionate conviction, abhorred the casual acceptance of the ministry as merely one of many acceptable occupations. To him it was "a sacred office which I venerate from the bottom of my heart as far superior to any other calling in the world."

Now he saw the most prominent members of the Moderate Party which was dominating the Church. The first of their kind, many years before, had been men in whom faith and theological scholarship were coupled with breadth of interests and liberality of thought. Through the years, moderation had degenerated to laxity and indifference. Among the prominent clergy, social charm and literary accomplishment often replaced religious fervour, and the lesser men, like William Mackenzie of Norman's home parish, could only compensate for their spiritual emptiness with cheerful conviviality. Now Norman was convinced that the qualities he deplored in Mackenzie were not simply an individual's faults, but a symptom of the dominant trend among ministers. Their way of life he loathed with all the scorn of his bitter disillusionment. Their subservience to their patrons and the State he proudly denounced.

In this view he was not alone. Such convictions, which had sent out thousands in secession from the Church, were disturbing many of his fellow students. At their lodgings they spent long hours in argument. Some felt that the ministry had lost its purpose, that their ideal had been shattered. Others were pleased to accept an assured income and an agreeable life. Still others insisted that even within a lax and worldly church a devout man could hold his course untouched. The college standards of scholarship in divinity were not high; there was little leadership from the faculty. Norman wanted none. Harshly he faced the facts; he made his decision; he acted. At the age of thirty-four, after six years of preparation, he renounced the ministry of the Church of Scotland.

In his later years he recaptured in a soliloquy his feelings on leaving Edinburgh. It is easy to suspect the profession of humility and the denial of pride, but under the cloak of words the real issue remains. "O Lord, I find that I have done forever with Edinburgh, in which I have passed very weary and yet most joyful days and nights. I would bless thee for all thy unmerited mercies to me both spiritual and providential. I am thought by some people strangely singular and by some others deeply fanatical, because I will not and dare not pronounce their Shibboleth. I am judged brutish, nay, proud and insolent and insensible to benefits and favours because I cannot obtain them by flattery, nor retain them by sinful complaisance. But thou knowest, O searcher of hearts, that were it enjoined by thee as my known duty, and accepted by men as their humble pleasure I would most cheerfully bow down and wash the feet not only of my superior and benevolent friends, but of my very prejudiced and malevolent enemies. But for all this glow of affection, I take the heavens to witness, that, had I no alternative, I should at once prefer being chained to the West India slave, enjoying full liberty of conscience, to being joined with the Scottish clergy in all their enjoyment under the present power of their disposition and the actual spirit of their administration."[3]

[3] McLeod, op. cit., p. 100.

CHAPTER FOUR

Contest in Ullapool

BEFORE HIS SECOND SESSION WAS ENDED, Norman had left Edinburgh. The Church was now closed to him, but he could still use his learning as a schoolmaster. He was hired by the Edinburgh Society for Promoting Christian Knowledge to teach at the village of Ullapool about thirty miles from his home. Ullapool was on Loch Broom, a lake so famous for its herring that some years earlier the British Fishing Company had established a business there and built some houses. From that time it had grown until there were nearly a hundred homes, not the poor huts of the northern straths, but solid stone buildings, many with slate roofs, set in attractive gardens. For the inhabitants, the catching and curing of fish ensured a reasonably stable income.

The prospects for the school were good. There would be nearly one hundred pupils, and the salary, paid partly by pupils' fees and partly through the parish minister, by the Society for Promoting Christian Knowledge, promised to be nearly seventy pounds, a large sum in comparison to Norman's previous earnings and to the standards of the community. In the summer of 1814, he moved Mary and their baby son John to Ullapool and they set up housekeeping, almost lavishly, with a servant, a pony and other luxuries, in one of the grey stone houses by the shore.

The school was immediately a success, but there was a foreshadowing of trouble since it was under the immediate jurisdiction of the parish minister, Dr. Ross. As his parish was large, he could seldom preach in Ullapool, and Norman was required, as his predecessors had been, to read the Scriptures to the villagers each Sunday and comment upon them. As in his home parish, his intensity and eloquence captured his hearers in Ullapool.

Dr. Ross, one of the outstanding Gaelic scholars of his time, a man whose intellect Norman freely admired, was fully in the tradition of the Moderate Party of the Church. His sermons were broad but not deep. Norman describes how in preaching on "Ye are the light of the world," "all the planetary system is at once in blaze as the scene of action—Hercules and Herschel, Neptune and Newton are all in motion." But, says Norman, "the name of a sinner or a Saviour would rarely occupy a place in his philosophical discourses."[1]

Although his unlearned parishioners listened in awe and admiration to the Doctor's knowledge, Norman saw it as a superficial display. He bluntly said so and did not attend the services. The Doctor, an irascible man, understandably annoyed by the attitude of the arrogant schoolmaster under his supervision, became violently excited during one of his rare sermons at Ullapool. He warned any of his hearers who supported Norman's religious services to leave the meeting and his ministry at once. He then ordered the people of the village to withdraw their children from Norman's school or to forfeit their church privileges if Norman continued to disobey him by not attending his services. The people all stood by Norman and refused to comply, except the chief elder who withdrew his son—no great loss, according to Norman, who, after many years of teaching, still remembered him as "the toughest twig that ever graced my drill." The Doctor, however, became so violent in his threats against the neighbourhood that Norman's resignation seemed the only solution. Norman faced the decision, he records, "with very tight struggles of mind between my sense of duty and desire of ease in my dear native land, and among my generous employers."

Before Norman had announced his resignation, Dr. Ross summoned him to appear before his Kirk session. It was a tense contest.[2] The Doctor accused him of keeping the people of Ullapool from attending his ministry. Norman insisted that their choice was free. The Doctor offered a compromise—"If you yourself should appear here now and then, even rarely, say once in a quarter, and show otherwise by your conversation and con-

[1] ibid., p. 299.

[2] The account of the contest with Dr. Ross and ensuing events appears in McLeod, *The Present Church of Scotland*, pp. 299-320.

duct your approbation of my ministry, I could freely indulge you. But your example beside your preaching is a stumbling block to them." "I don't call my service 'preaching,'" said Norman. The contest then turned to Norman's right to explain the Scriptures. Norman, in his defence, quoted the Biblical passage, "As every man hath received the gift, even so minister the same one to another, as good stewards...." Here the impasse was complete. The Doctor insisted that Norman was claiming some extraordinary spiritual gift; Norman declared that the words referred to every individual. Neither ever yielded.

There was no winner in the long day's argument, but the authority was all the Doctor's. He offered Norman twenty days of grace before he should be deprived of the school. Norman strode from the house.

Twenty years later he vividly recalled what happened that night. "It rained in such an extraordinary manner as swelled the river which runs alongside the meeting-house and the manse; and so intervened my intended return home that evening. I had left my pony on the other side; and the Doctor's best horse could not now cross me over. I stopped at the river's side, in anxious but vain expectation of getting home, till I was perfectly drenched and pitch-dark night necessitated my return to shelter. In great confusion of face I popped into the Doctor's kitchen for there was no other house near me. Happily there was no person there at the time; and I tumbled my poor carcass into an empty bed, not far from the warmth of a good fire, where I intended to coop concealed till the morning, for it was in April. But alas, I was soon detected by the servants, who immediately spread the alarm through the manse; in consequence of which the generous Doctor sent a message for me to the parlour, where his Reverence and his lady, with a few more, sat at tea; among whom was one of his elders, a select member of the Session.

"I dare say, in truth, in my life of sixty, I never felt so much reluctance and embarrassment at any other invitation as arrested the feelings of my soul at that moment.... The good Doctor and his Elder who had fought such a hot and hectoring battle with me through the day, upon some of the most serious and sublime subjects possible were now as free and frivolous at every chitchat, at their tea and toddy, as little children! I might also by this providence learn more of my own weakness. For though my very soul was disgusted at the vanity and frivolity of my prosecutors, yet the present shame of being chargeable of ill manners or indecorum among superiors at once disarmed the ordinary active exercise of my religious zeal and merited reflection on the unbecoming conference and conduct of my associates, so as in a degree to yield, though most reluctantly and, I dare say, very awkwardly, to the current pulse of the company. Fruitless and formal family worship served at last to close the scene. And the good Doctor himself in order to show his utmost condescension and kindness, introduced me to my bedroom with a flaming candle in each hand—in their silver sockets; and in the most pleasant and placid manner, bade me good night."

While Norman was suffering the hardships of his comfortable night, Mary, too anxious to wait at home, was plodding alone in the darkness toward him, hoping every moment for the sound of the pony's hooves. Delicate as she was, she walked the nine rough miles till she reached the river and heard from the neighbour who took her in that Norman was safe. It was the first of many times that Mary's delicate body would suffer for Norman's spirit—this would become the pattern of their life.

Neither kindness nor opposition influenced Norman; he carried on his school and his Sunday services as usual until the twenty days were over. Then the Doctor locked the school and chapel and took the key. On Sundays the villagers still collected about Norman to hear his teaching.

It had been an expensive year for the McLeods. There had been the expense of setting up a home, in which, because of Norman's expected salary, they had incurred debts. In addition to his pupils' fees, Norman was to receive twenty-five pounds from the Society for Promoting Christian Knowledge. This sum, which was to be paid through the parish minister, Dr. Ross refused to pay. Now, having lost his position and one-third of his salary, Norman had only his old trade as a fisherman.

Before he could return to it he was to have two more encounters with Dr. Ross. One was caused by a load of wood. That summer Dr. Ross and his neighbour were having land cleared for pasture. They offered that anyone cutting trees on their land could have, in return for work, one-half of the wood he cut. When Norman's cousin who was visiting him wanted some of this wood, Norman went with him to get it and agreed to keep the wood temporarily piled by his house until the cousin could return for it.

Meanwhile, Norman and Mary decided that their baby son, John, who had been born a few months before, should be taken to the Loch Carron communion for baptism. Rev. Lachlan McKenzie was the parish minister. He was Norman's relative, and although Norman had not met him, he had heard much of McKenzie's piety. He felt sure that he could in good conscience accept from him the baptism of his son. So, over forty miles of moss and mountain they carried little John to Loch Carron.

McKenzie had already invited Dr. Ross to his services. Now he planned that the two men would meet in his study and be reconciled. But in his simple good will he had underestimated the antagonists. Ross's hot temper and Norman's harsh obstinacy made compromise impossible. So baby John, who could have no sacrament without the consent of his father's parish minister, was carried home unbaptized.

At home there was another surprise. In the window was a summons from Dr. Ross, with a charge of 150 pounds for stealing the pile of wood. Norman must pay or go to prison. He at once sent for his cousin. Cousin John had the wood valued by arbiters who estimated it at 7s. Unjust though the charge appeared to the community, there was no way of appealing to the Doctor. Norman and his cousin turned to their old landlord, Squire McDonald of Loch Inver, under whose proprietary they had grown up and had first held land. He immediately acted on their behalf, but Norman still had to appear in court in Dingwall.

To Norman, this charge, false and ridiculous though he knew it to be, was a keener blow than the loss of his school. As he recalled, "None ignorant of the simplicity of our Highlanders in those times, and of the rarity of legal prosecution—especially remote from public and borough towns—can form but very faint ideas of the natural confusion, then commonly attendant on a summons, particularly like ours, for alleged vil-

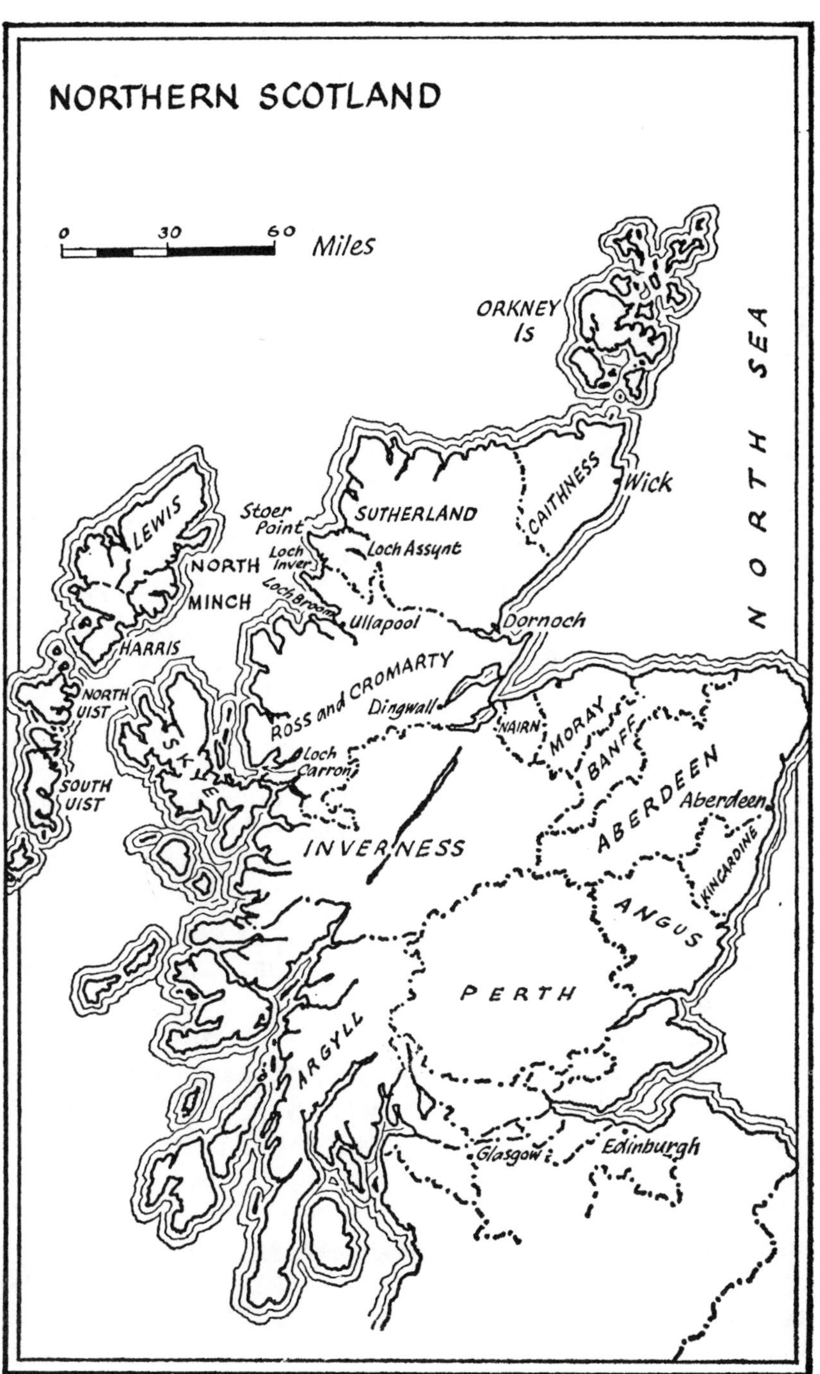
NORTHERN SCOTLAND
0
30
60
Miles
ORKNEY Is
NORTH SEA
Wick
CAITHNESS
SUTHERLAND
Stoer Point
Loch Assynt
Loch Inver
LEWIS
NORTH MINCH
Loch Broom
Ullapool
Dornoch
HARRIS
ROSS and CROMARTY
Dingwall
NORTH UIST
NAIRN
MORAY
BANFF
SKYE
Loch Carron
SOUTH UIST
ABERDEEN
Aberdeen
INVERNESS
KINCARDINE
ANGUS
PERTH
ARGYLL
Glasgow
Edinburgh

lainy or felony! In my case, being keenly tender of my religious character—and then placed in a comparatively strange situation—I certainly experienced the full measure of the smart."

These were anxious days. Norman had set himself up as a critic of the Church's ministers. For these principles he had given up a university degree and a career in the ministry, he had given up the comfortable security of his teaching position. He could justify himself only if, as an individual, he was above reproach. His neighbours knew that he was an innocent victim, but what of the people at a distance if they were to hear that the righteous Norman McLeod had been jailed for stealing a load of wood?

From Friday morning till dusk on Saturday Norman waited in Dingwall to see the Doctor's attorney. When they finally met they had a pleasant talk and the lawyer was readily convinced of Norman's innocence. In his excitement and relief, Norman thought only of the anxious people waiting for him at home. The rainy night was closing in, and forty miles of moor and hill were before him, but he strode confidently on until at sunrise Sunday morning he reached home and the friends who had watched all night.

Now Norman's reputation was secure. He triumphed like an Old Testament hero, confident that the Lord was on his side, and that those who had conspired against him would, even in this world, be duly punished. He needed all his assurance; there was a hard winter ahead. Mary, worn out by the worry and confusion of the year, became desperately ill. Norman had to give up his plans of going away to find work, and stay home to look after little John and his baby brother, Donald, and go still more deeply into debt. It was a testing time for his principles—even his sincere friends accused him of "needless scrupulosity of conscience" and "illiberal religious sentiments." They pointed out that an individual could still be a good Christian without forfeiting the good will of the clergy. An outward compromise was not for Norman. He still would state his views, still the debts mounted, the winter's supplies were used up, and Mary was ill.

Through a mutual acquaintance, Dr. Ross offered him a boll (six bushels) of his oatmeal if he should send for it. Norman thanked him, but firmly refused. Dr. Ross sent the meal, however, and the messenger poured it into an empty cask which he found in a closet, and left the house before Norman's return. Norman decided to "make no further bustle" on the subject and allowed his family to use the flour. He spent many days suspiciously analysing the purpose of the gift.

These conflicts with Dr. Ross were to affect Norman's whole life. He left Edinburgh with a strong disapproval of general trends among the clergy. Now he had a deep personal resentment. To the passion of a rebel he added the querulousness of a martyr. Long after, he attributed his coming to North America to the "prosecution if not the persecution of that man."

It was in this mood that he began to consider emigration—not as an exciting adventure but as a last resort. He was thirty-six years old and not yet started on a career. In Scotland he had closed all the doors against himself—while the Church controlled the schools there would be no future for him there.

Since he was a child he had heard stories of the freedom, the fertility, the riches, the easy life in North America. As a man, from the sailors in Aberdeen, from friends who had emigrated, and from his reading, he had learned the other side of the story. He knew that life would not be easy; ease he had always despised. Riches he could scorn for principle's sake though he respected them as one does who has struggled for subsistence. He felt fully confident in trusting himself with absolute freedom. This he could surely find in the scattered settlements of America, far from the control of an established church. As spring came and Mary's health returned he began to look westward.

First he must pay their debts. Since he had to earn the highest possible wages, the local fisheries would not suffice. Instead he went to Wick, centre of the dangerous east coast fisheries of Caithness. Only expert fishermen, sometimes as many as ten thousand from all over England and Scotland, came to Wick for the fishing season. The fishing was excellent, markets were sure, wages were high. Norman was free of debt by the end of the year.

Now he could save for his passage to North America, and

for the money to keep Mary and their children during the year until they could join him. This he achieved, and in July 1817 he sailed from Loch Broom on the barque *Frances Ann* for Pictou, Nova Scotia.

CHAPTER FIVE

Norman's *Ark*

THE FOUR HUNDRED PEOPLE aboard the *Frances Ann* crowded the deck, marking each croft, naming the fishing boats as they passed, memorizing the familiar pattern of the shore. Their dreams of America might be bright, but at that moment they were altogether exiles. With Celtic melancholy they treasured the sad satisfaction of the hour. "Return, return, return we never"—from the ship the words of McCrimmon's lament echoed against the hills.

They had known the unpredictable perils of the sea, but few of them had ever been out of the sight of land. When the thin purple line of the Irish coast had finally dissolved into the horizon, even the most confident wondered if they had done the right thing, and the others gave way to their fears.

There was comfort then in Norman's daily services of prayer. Some of the passengers had known him in Ullapool or in his home parish of Assynt, and had already fallen under the spell of his oratory and felt the conviction of his mission. The others saw a tall, spare man, bronzed and hardened by his fishing days at Wick, moving about the deck with easy assurance, even giving a competent hand with the ropes, stern with the men who were drowning the dull hours in whisky, gentle with the honest fears of others. They heard this man reading the familiar psalms, and saying the words which had comforted and inspired them at home. From him came assurance. As the days passed they began almost imperceptibly to change from a confusion of individuals sharing only a common loss into a body of people with a destination.

The same thing happened to Norman. He embarked on the voyage a self-made exile. Now, buoyed up by the dependence of his fellow passengers, he was facing the new world with a purpose. For more than ten years he had been a rebel; in America he could become a builder.

His testing time came suddenly. When they were about four weeks out, the *Frances Ann* was caught in a violent gale. She sprang a leak. All hands took turns at the pumps, every man among the passengers lent a hand, but still the sea was defeating them. The captain summoned all the passengers, he told them the danger, he stated that they would put back for the coast of Ireland. The people, weak from seasickness, all their fears revived by this new peril, were superstitiously sure that their voyage was ill-omened. All were willing to turn back. Norman said "No."

With his old recklessness he challenged them—the expert seamen and his newly-won followers. On their response hung possibly their survival, certainly his fate as a leader. The captain stormed, he threatened to put Norman in irons. The people, huddled in helpless little groups, watched the antagonists. The captain raged at the interference of an ignorant preacher; Norman, sternly calm, demonstrated with mathematical precision that they were nearer to Nova Scotia than to Ireland. Then he turned to the people. He told them, legend relates, that he had seen a vision, that if they turned back they were lost. Visions in a mystical sense do not accord with Norman's practical realism, but how else could he explain his sense of destiny, or translate his mathematical calculations to an ignorant mob? Against their superstitious fear he placed his vision. The anxious faces watched him. He waited. Gradually from the silent people came murmurs of assent. Norman turned to the captain. "You'll hang for this," the captain muttered as he turned back to the bridge—to keep the ship on her course for Nova Scotia.

With Norman's supervision every available blanket was requisitioned from the passengers and stuffed into the leak. The male passengers had a regular schedule at the pumps. The wind stayed in the east, each day brought them nearer. They sighted Newfoundland, then the wooded highlands of Cape Breton. At last the deep green line of the shore was broken by pale patches of clearings, wisps of smoke merged with the hazy September sky. The harbour of Pictou opened before them. The captain came to Norman. "You're a much better navigator than I am, Mr. McLeod." "It was the Lord's doing," said Norman.

In awe the newcomers gazed at the dark green hills. The giant oaks and pines faced them in a seemingly impenetrable barrier. They thought of the birch and alder scattered in spindly patches back home. The forest was discouraging, but the hills were gentler here, their softly rounded lines enfolding the blue haven of the harbour. The water spread smooth and wide before them, separated by the hills into the three streams which they would soon know as East, West and Middle Rivers. Near the mouth of the East River there seemed to be a gigantic raft; as they went up the harbour, it became logs, thousands of logs. By the shore, too, were piles of logs larger and longer than they had ever seen. On the wharves men were unloading barrels of herring, hogsheads of molasses and rum. Between the cargo vessels little rowboats pushed in and out. From the deck of the *Frances Ann* the newcomers could look down into their cargoes—the casks, jugs and parcels which the settlers were carrying home to their coastal farms. Beyond the ships stood the collection of stores and houses that was the village of Pictou. A few solid stone buildings looked familiar and secure, but the rest were of wood, some of them grey from twenty years' weathering, others harshly new.

Through the village and down the paths from the hillside homes, people were hurrying to the dock to wait for the *Frances Ann*. Almost every ship brought to the Highlanders of Pictou relatives or friends from Scotland. "Is it yourself, Duncan?"; "Jamie, it's the big man you are!"; "Come away, Margaret, lass, let me take the bairn." With familiar voices and careful restraint of words they took the travellers home. There were many for whom no old friends waited, but the lines of kinship and the parish loyalties were strong. Strangers took them to find people from their old districts or offered lodging until the newcomers could continue to their destinations inland, or send word of their arrival to their kinsmen farther away.

The people were familiar, but the place was like nothing they had known. Pictou was an American frontier settlement, riding high on the biggest boom it would ever see. Captain

Lowden had begun shipbuilding there in the 1790s, and when the European war closed the Baltic to Britain, the lumber business surged ahead. Pictou was one of Britain's best sources of timber. Prices skyrocketed. From 1800 to 1820, exports from Pictou, principally lumber, averaged one hundred thousand pounds a year. Every able-bodied man was somehow in the lumber business.

Lumber was available everywhere—even the farms which had been settled thirty years before had most of their acreage yet to clear. But this time of high prices, good wages and a great demand for lumber did not mean that the land was being systematically cleared and improved. Only the best logs were taken out, the brush and stumps remained and the small trees were left standing. Farmers snatched a few days in the spring to sow and a few days in the autumn to harvest the grain on their cleared patches of land, but they took little time to clear more. After harvest many of them went inland for the winter to the steady wages and free life of the lumber camps. For the first time in Pictou they traded with money instead of goods. Before they were ready, the war had forced them away from pioneer self-sufficiency. Transferred almost overnight from privation to plenty, the workers spent lavishly. For the merchants and tavern keepers times were good.

Rum was pouring in from the West Indies. There were few restrictions and plenty of money. Hard drinking was the rule. Every job carried a daily rum allowance of two or three glasses. In almost every home, with the decanter always on a corner of the dinner table, at least half a puncheon of rum would be consumed in the winter. In the woods, even with a daily allowance of two glasses of rum, a man could often be employed all winter at five shillings a day yet still be in debt in the spring though he had bought little else but rum.

So money flowed through the community, but the stores and warehouses which it provided were not the only symbols of life in Pictou. In 1786 the Presbyterian Church had sent Dr. James McGregor to the district. It was to a congregation which heckled, whistled and tried to shout him down that he had begun his ministry. Before the end of his first winter, some of the retired army officers who had been settled at Pictou since the end of the American war, threatened to shoot him and burn his house. The French war drained off these troublemakers, but even before they had gone, the character and temperament of James McGregor had established him as an ideal pioneer missionary. Audacious, powerful, physically strong, he set himself no limits. He tramped thousands of miles through the woods, visited lonely settlements even in Prince Edward Island and Cape Breton, preached tirelessly in Gaelic and in English. He was the comfort, reproach, terror, inspiration of his vast territory.

For nearly ten years he worked alone. Then he was joined by the Rev. Duncan Ross, and in 1803 by Rev. Thomas McCulloch, writer, controversialist and educator, whose plans for higher learning in the community issued, the year of Norman's arrival, in the founding of Pictou Academy.

All these men were ministers of groups dissenting from the Established Church of Scotland, and with them into the new world they carried the old antagonisms. When increasing numbers of immigrants arrived from Highland parishes which were still attached to the Established Church the newcomers began to clamour for ministers of their own denomination. They also believed, erroneously, that a minister of the Established Church would be paid by the State and they would be free of responsibility for his salary. In 1817, in answer to their pleas, Rev. Donald Fraser came to them from the Isle of Mull.

So, in the year of Norman's arrival, the familiar Scottish strife was, with Mr. Fraser, transplanted to Pictou. With Fraser's successors, who were typical of the moderate clergy of Scotland, it grew and produced a conflict which reached into every part of the county and often separated friends and families. It was not strange that these antagonisms should have survived, every other element in their lives had to be adapted to their new environment, only with these narrow sectarian ties could individuals keep their old identity. For some, then, they became doubly precious. Norman soon realized that freedom from conflict, criticism and control was not to be found in Pictou.

While he was learning about the life of Pictou, he was also getting settled, on land between the West and Middle rivers, ironically, near Lochbroom, namesake of the scene of his Scottish troubles. Since there were at least 12,000 people now living in Pictou county, most of the best and most convenient sites had been taken up. The newcomers of the *Frances Ann* would have liked to settle in a group and would undoubtedly have found in their enriched admiration for Norman the centre of such a settlement. Instead they had to take the scattered lots which were still available. But, even among strangers, it was an unwritten rule that any neighbours helped a new settler build his cabin. Round logs, undressed, fifteen to twenty feet long, were used, and the seams between were closed with moss or clay. Even a man of Norman's tremendous strength needed experienced help. His experience in the hewing of Dr. Ross's controversial alders at the old Lochbroom was of little value in the woods of Nova Scotia.

In Pictou county every settler began with an axe and a hoe. With the axe he blazed a trail from his neighbour's cabin to his own, he felled the trees and lopped off the branches. In the spring he burned all the wood that was not needed, and in the cleared space sowed wheat and covered it with the hoe. With the hoe he also planted hills of potatoes. Rich with vegetable mould from centuries of decayed leaves and the ashes from burned wood, the soil was phenomenally fertile. For the new settler, results were quick in a good year.

Even the best results meant only the bare necessities of life. The first homes of each group of new settlers probably had changed little from those which James McGregor described when he first came to Pictou: "Their furniture was of the rudest description; frequently a block of wood or a rude bench, made out of a slab, in which four sticks had been inverted as legs, served for chairs or table. Their food was commonly served up in wooden dishes or wooden plates and eaten with wooden spoons, except when, discarding such interventions, they adopted the more direct method of gathering around the pot of potatoes on the floor. And among the newcomers, at least, a little straw formed the only bed."[1]

During the week, Norman cleared his land and on Sundays

[1] Patterson, George, ed., *Memoir of the Rev. James McGregor*, p. 82.

If the wishes of the people concerned should succeed the situation of the School houses would, of
Course, be fixed by the Board of Commissioners thro'
the medium of some proper persons in our neighbourhood, or at the mutual decision of the applicants
themselves.

I am Revd & dear Sir,

Your Obt Servt

N. McLeod

Rev. Norman McLeod; his handwriting in an 1840 letter quoted in Chapter 8

The coast of Assynt in Scotland: Clachtoll Bay near Stoer

St. Ann's Harbour
in Cape Breton Island
from A. F. Church's map of
Victoria County, circa 1864

Two views of St. Ann's Bay, Cape Breton Island.

Left: The granite millstone monument to Rev. Norman McLeod. It stands at the head of St. Ann's Harbour, on what was Norman's land, site of the present-day Gaelic College of Celtic Arts & Crafts. The English inscription is on page 1. The Gaelic reads: "Threòraich e a shluagh 's an àite so 'n a linn fhéin mar mhinistear, maighistir-sgoile, 's fear-lagha. Rugadh e an Rudha Stòrr, an Asaint, an Albainn. Thàinig e gu Pictou 's a' bhliadhna 1817, 's sheòl e le a chuideachd gu St. Ann an 1820, far an d'fhuirich iad gu ruige 1851, 'n uair a dh' fhalbh iad an toiseach gu Australia, is mu dheireadh gu New Zealand."

he preached at his own cabin. When his following increased, Mr. Ross relinquished to him his church at Middle River. Of his preaching, George Patterson, the county historian, gives the outsiders' viewpoint: "Those who heard him at this time describe his preaching as consisting of torrents of abuse against all religious bodies, and even against individuals, the like of which they had never heard and which were perfectly indescribable. He had never been licensed or ordained, but regarded himself as under higher influences than the ministers of any church....

"But though so wildly fanatical, he was a man of great power, and gained an influence over a large portion of the Highlanders, such as no man in the county possessed.... His influence extended to many in almost every part of the county, and by his followers he was regarded with unbounded devotion."[2]

There is no record of his relationship with Dr. McGregor, though Norman later spoke favourably of him. A few years after Norman had left Pictou and returned only to visit his followers, Dr. McGregor reported to a Scottish society: "There is a fourfold zeal in Pictou; First, zeal for the Established Church of Scotland; in some this zeal is wonderfully strong. Secondly, zeal for the Presbyterian Church of Nova Scotia [formed of the union of dissenting Presbyterians in 1817]. Thirdly, zeal for lukewarmness; and this party are so earnestly set upon it that neither of the foregoing parties have been able to move them. Fourthly, zeal for Norman McLeod. The above gentleman [another Pictou minister, probably Rev. Donald Fraser] knows now, that numbers who had received tokens of admission to the Lord's Table, at his last Sacrament, hearing on Saturday evening that Norman was come back to Pictou, left the Sacrament, and travelled through the night to hear him preach, next day, in a distant part of the district. He may also know that Norman will get three hearers to his one; and that people will go much farther to hear him than any minister in Pictou. And who is Norman? A self-made preacher who declares that there is not a minister of Christ in all the Church of Scotland."[3]

Although he decried the recklessness of the new country

2 Patterson, George, *History of the County of Pictou*, p. 319.
3 Patterson, George, ed., *Remains of the Rev. James McGregor*, p. 258.

and the shallowness of the clergy imported from Scotland, Norman continued to write to his friends in his native parish, urging them to emigrate. He could see that the fertility of the soil and the unclaimed lands offered to farmers an opportunity which would be forever denied them in the Highlands. Certainly, too, although he was aware of his powerful leadership, he was also aware of the other influences of their new country on his scattered people, leading them from the life which he would choose for them. He saw that, as soon as possible, they needed more strong men who shared his own firm beliefs.

He had so interested his friends in Assynt that when, in the early spring of 1818, Captain Hector McKenzie came to the parish to enlist passengers for America, he readily found one hundred and fifty to sail with him on the *Perseverance* in July. Among these emigrants were some of Norman's boyhood friends: Donald McLeod (known as "the Squire"), Norman McDonald, and the brothers Alex, Donald and John Munro. Unlike most of Norman's first Pictou followers, many of whom could not read or write, these were competent businessmen, some of them with a classical education. They were the men that a new settlement would need.

At Pictou they found no hope of a consolidated settlement. The passengers scattered where land was still available and where they had friends. Few could be near Norman or his church.

To Norman, instinctively dependent on the physical closeness of the tribe, separation seemed perilous. Only in their proximity as well as in their unity could there be a barrier against the free life of the frontier—a life which, for his people, Norman feared. He had come to Pictou confident in his own ability to use freedom from official restraint. That others, too, were looking for freedom and would inevitably use it in different ways he did not understand or tolerate. So, years later, he wrote: "Pictou had been preparing for evil days before I first left it; and in truth it was my concern on that ground that made me loth & fearful at the time to remain any longer within its boundaries. I experienced an awful & uncommon dread on my heart & spirit concerning the increasing audacity and formality of the inhabitants, as well as the approaching appearance of the tokens of God's displeasure, which I have never seen reason before now to tell but to a few intimate friends.... I know not the comparison of Pictou in the whole land for shameless & daring wickedness."[4] He mentions the places about New Glasgow and "the filthiness prevalent there, particularly at the shipping-place...." "Dishonest & deceitful modes of transaction, particularly in lands & horses were some of the first enormities that arrested my own mind with disgust & alarm, after my landing in that quarter; especially on finding that that wicked habit was carried on so generally, without a blush of shame, even among the oldest and most glaring professors of religion, as well as the loosest & wildest set of young men in the country. Wild jest, or malignant scorn at any testimony, by precept or practice, any wise reflecting on the current sentiments or conduct of these scorners has for a long time been another gloomy sign of the place. It was at the bridge & forge of West River that I first ever heard profane swearing by the awful name of the Holy Ghost."[5]

As the scene of a settlement which Norman could mould or lead, the Pictou district seemed impossible. Neither would he willingly bring up in its atmosphere his three little sons, who, with their mother, had arrived that summer. It was not for him to compromise, or to share in the improvement of the community. His was not the zeal of Dr. McGregor who went out to search for men. Instead all his impulse was to withdraw the faithful from the menace of the worldly community. For his own people he reserved an assurance and a tenderness which won in return a devotion, almost an adoration, incomprehensible to outsiders. Sure in his own sufficiency he built around them like a thorny hedge his fierce denunciation of other clergy, and his brutal castigation of all ways that were not his own. But he still required a place where, in a homogeneous settlement, he would not need to spend all his force in holding a people together, but could direct it toward the shaping of their life into his interpretation of the divine plan.

[4] Harvey, D. C., ed., *Letters of the Rev. Norman McLeod*, p. 10.
[5] ibid., p. 11.

In his second year at Pictou, Norman was invited by a settlement of Highlanders in the United States to come to be their minister. Tradition suggests that this was in Ohio. After the War of 1812, the rapid growth of the Presbyterian Church there was creating an enormous demand for missionaries to go westward with the settlers and for pastors to take charge of the newly-built churches. Many years later, Norman still corresponded with a friend in New Lisbon, Ohio, but since the Presbyterian Church in that village had a settled minister from 1807 to 1839 it seems unlikely that he was invited there. Another suggestion names Hamilton, Ohio. Whether he had a specific call to the vicinity of either of these villages, or whether his plan was merely in accord with the well-known demand for ministers in the new State, Norman determined to leave for Ohio.

It was a test of his growing power. He asked his people to go with him to Ohio. Once again he acted alone—his going was not dependent on their support. For their going his presence would be the reward. There were other possible advantages, but the vague promise of a milder climate and better land would scarcely make people who had just come 2,000 miles to a strange country pack up to move once more. Even harder it would be for those who had endured the first years of settlement to think of beginning again. It would mean, too, leaving the sea which they had known for generations to go to a forest-bound land where they could not practise the blend of fishing and farming which was their familiar way of life. There must have been many households where argument raged long into the night, but powerful was the spell of Norman McLeod. Many decided to go.

The plan, according to legend, was that they should sail along the Atlantic coast, into the Gulf of Mexico to the mouth of the Mississippi, then up the great river to the Ohio. On the map it appears impractical, but to these men who had grown up on the rocky coast of Sutherland a thousand miles of coastal navigation must have seemed less daunting than a hundred through the strange dark forest. It is possible, of course, that they may have planned to go by ship only to New York and from there to follow the immigrant trail westward. For either plan they had to have a boat. This required not only loyalty but money. From Norman's friends it came—principally from the Munro brothers and the other recent arrivals from Scotland.

The newcomers had built only the fishing boats with which they had earned their summer wages at Loch Inver, but among the older settlers were men who had worked in the Pictou shipyards. At Middle River Point they laid the keel of the little schooner. Through spring and summer as the work went on the neighbours jeered. Norman had foretold disaster to frivolous Pictou; now as he prepared his vessel against the day of destruction the people of Pictou derisively named it the "Ark." The name was good-naturedly adopted by Norman's followers who were also winning their own distinctive name of "Normanites."

It was decided that on this reconnoitring voyage only a group of the men would go. After they had reached their destination they could prepare homes before the ship returned for their friends and families. In September, 1819, the eighteen-ton schooner was ready, furnished with provisions, charts and compasses and all the necessary supplies for the long voyage. Norman appointed Norman McDonald navigator, "Squire" McLeod sailing master, Hugh Matheson chief officer. The Squire's son, John McLeod (later called "Arichat" from an association with the Cape Breton fishing village), Norman McDonald's son Alex and a few others made up the crew. The women with their young children prepared to face their first Nova Scotian winter alone.

The *Ark* sailed bravely out of Pictou harbour. Since this, the first ship they had built, was as yet untried in the open sea, they decided to test her by following the Cape Breton coastline around Cape North instead of crossing directly through the Strait of Canso into the September gales of the North Atlantic. Slowly they sailed along in the shelter of the island, anchoring in little harbours at night, moving northward by day below the sheer cliffs of the western shore. The *Ark* was handling well, but they were in no hurry to face the open Atlantic. For Norman, after two years in the woods it was a joy to be at sea. They explored the coast and stopped to fish. After they had rounded Cape North, they had to fight a rougher sea, and on a calm sunny afternoon they were glad to stop to fish near the mouth of St. Ann's harbour. They got a good catch of cod, and, well satisfied, anchored for the night just within the harbour mouth.

They looked inland in the morning sunshine. The calm blue waters were encircled by heavy spruce interlaced with the silver lines of birches, softened by the golden haze of the autumn woods. A circle of low mountains enclosed them. Slowly they sailed the six miles to the head of the bay. The waters were teeming with fish. They landed; they consulted briefly; they decided to stay.

Each man selected a location along the shore and began to clear a plot of ground for spring work. They put up the walls of shanties to be ready for their families in the spring. When these preparations were finished, they returned to Pictou for the winter. They sold the *Ark* to one of its shareholders, Alex Munro. Each of the partners began to prepare a small boat to carry his family to Cape Breton.

How Norman reconciled his mission to Ohio with the decision to remain at St. Ann's has never been explained. In those moments of discussion on the beach at St. Ann's the goal simply changed. Perhaps he now had enough experience as a leader to know how far he could ask men's loyalty. Perhaps the discovery of a beautiful, potentially prosperous site almost empty of settlers truly seemed a dispensation of Providence. Perhaps he had realized that he could not leave the sea. For the first time since his recognition as a leader he was making a decision alone with old friends. These men would not be persuaded by visions. Their leader had to be reasonable. In that moment on the beach Norman took the first step that was neither in rebellion nor in anger toward the community that he must build. He returned to Pictou with a new plan, still the acknowledged leader, to prepare for a new destiny at St. Ann's.

CHAPTER SIX

A Haven at St. Ann's

THROUGH THE WINTER of 1819 the explorers of St. Ann's worked at the building of their boats. Small in comparison to the *Ark*, each was large enough to carry a family for the relatively short distance to St. Ann's. Murdoch McDonald, who, as a twelve-year-old boy, helped his father, Norman, in the building of their boat, later described them as "what we would call life-boats." By the end of April, the little fleet at Middle River was ready for the migration.

As well as the passengers and their small supplies of food and clothing, tools, household equipment and even some livestock were crowded into the seven boats. Together they made their way through Pictou harbour. This time there were no jeers. Many of the spectators smiled with relief, or, daringly, cheered. They were finally rid of the scornful castigations of Norman McLeod; surely they would hear him no more from the wilderness of Cape Breton. The faces of others showed the sense of loss which would soon send them after him. Murdoch McDonald's grandfather, who had been in the Pictou district for fifteen years, saw his son-in-law, who had come only the year before and had already taken part in the strange expedition of the *Ark*, now carrying off his whole family in the train of Norman McLeod. There were others, too, who shook their heads.

The boats were to keep together on their course around Cape George to the Strait of Canso, but they reckoned without the northeasterly winds and the heavy seas beyond the shelter of the cape. There the storm had them at its mercy. Caught by the gale, Norman's boat, the largest of the fleet, was pushed helpless across Northumberland Strait, to be finally driven ashore on Prince Edward Island. The boat was unharmed; the passengers wearily stumbled toward shelter. At once there was help, from Father McEachern, the Roman Catholic priest who was soon to become Bishop of Prince Edward Island. As a young man, thirty years before, Angus McEachern had himself led a shipload of Highlanders from their homes in North Uist to begin a new settlement on St. John's Island (later called Prince Edward Island). In the years between, Scottish Roman Catholics under his direction had poured into the mainland of Nova Scotia in the vicinity of Cape George, built churches, and founded the town of Antigonish. Now the bishop met his fellow adventurer with friendly concern and took him and his family into his own house. For years Norman recalled his kindly hospitality. His followers noticed that, although he might deplore the doctrines of the Roman Catholic Church, he never thereafter denounced its priests.

The other boats were also seeking refuge. "Squire" McLeod's, forced back toward Pictou, landed at Arisaig Pier, then called "Priest's Wharf," since Arisaig was the site of the first Roman Catholic church in the area, and their priest had regularly come to them from the Island. Norman McDonald's boat, with seven persons aboard, was being driven ashore east of Cape George when a dozen men who were watching met her in the surf and hauled her in to safety. The McDonalds remained ashore there for two days. Then the Squire's boat joined them, and together they went on through the Strait of Canso to St. Peter's. There they waited, watching anxiously for the others. One by one the little boats appeared, scarred by the storm. Norman McLeod, from his distant haven in Prince Edward Island, was the last to come.

In turn the boats were hauled across the half-mile isthmus now cut by St. Peter's Canal. Then, reloaded, they made their way through the Bras d'Or lake. The ice had gone and the blue waters were a deepened echo of the spring sky. The northeast wind was chill and the snow still lingered in white patches under the heavy spruces, but the buds were casting a rosy haze about the maples, and, in mossy sheltered places on the shore were the fragrant pink clusters of the trailing arbutus. Only the travellers' voices, the splash of their oars, and the whirr of startled birds broke the silence of the lake.

Occasionally as they neared the Grand Narrows, the north

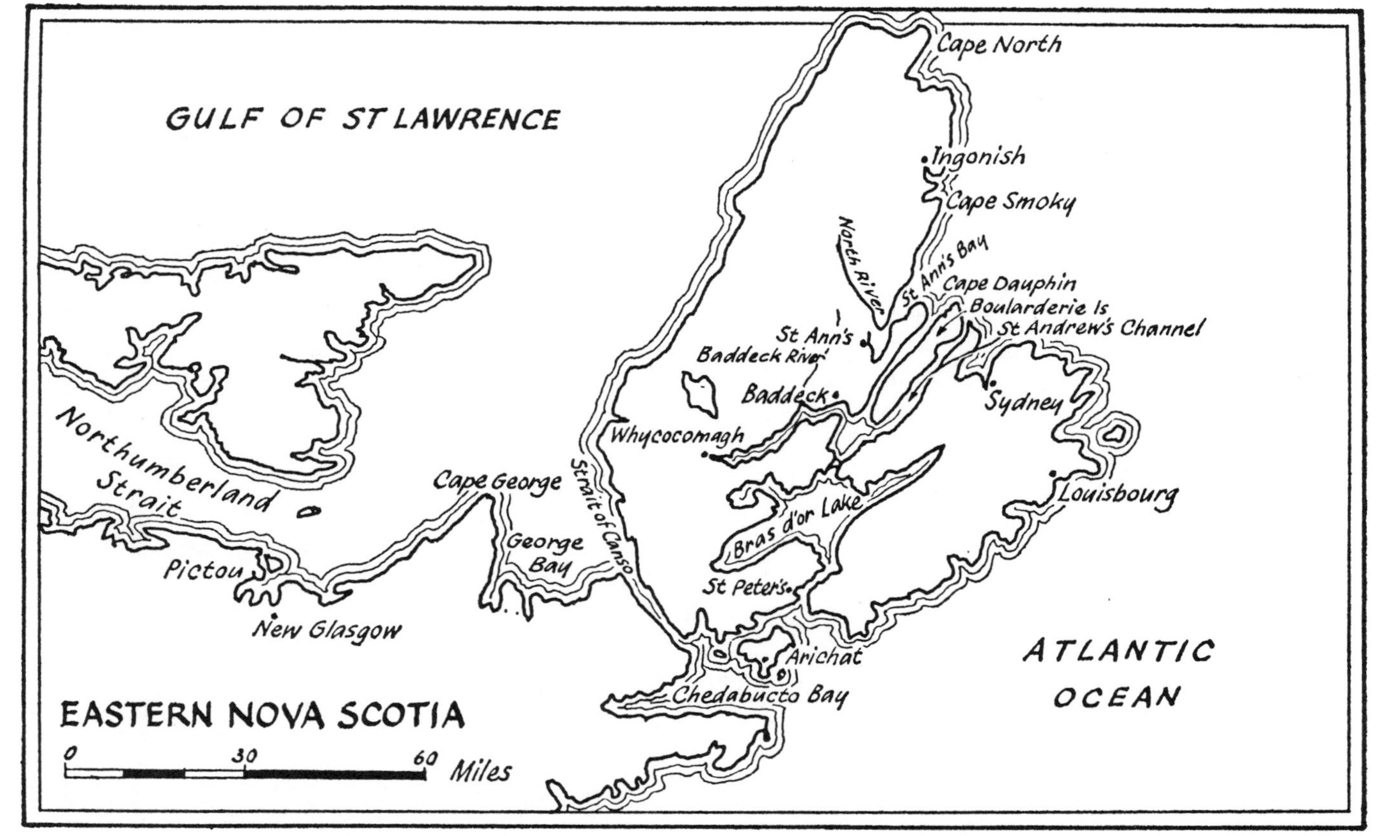
GULF OF ST LAWRENCE
Cape North
Ingonish
Cape Smoky
North River
St Ann's Bay
Cape Dauphin
Boularderie Is
St Andrew's Channel
St Ann's
Baddeck River
Baddeck
Sydney
Whycocomagh
Louisbourg
Bras d'or Lake
St Peter's
Arichat
Chedabucto Bay
Strait of Canso
Cape George
George Bay
Northumberland Strait
Pictou
New Glasgow
ATLANTIC OCEAN
EASTERN NOVA SCOTIA
0
30
60
Miles

wind brought the sound of a settler's axe, and as they entered the narrow strait they were surprised to discover on the shore a tiny Catholic church, and to see, drifting among the trees, the wisps of smoke that meant life in the wilderness. As they rowed along St. Andrew's Channel they heard the mingled noises of a settlement—the pounding of a hammer, the barking of dogs, the clang of iron on a blacksmith's anvil. At Baddeck and the promontory of Washabuck were barns and houses in patches of clearing and friendly voices calling from the shore. But soon the people and their cheerful sounds were behind them, and as they came to Boularderie Island and followed the Great Bras d'Or along its northern shore only the forbidding darkness of the woods rose from the water's edge.

On May 20th, 1820, in brilliant sunshine, Norman McDonald guided his boat around Cape Dauphin. He continued into St. Ann's Bay, and at the narrow entrance to the harbour, beached the boat on the southern shore. There, on the site of the present village of Englishtown, some fisherfolk had houses. They had been watching and waving from their doorsteps as the boat came near.

As they landed, the children came running down to the shore, and old John Roberts, hurrying with them, to invite the McDonald family to his house for the night. Soon the roll call of the little fleet was complete—"Squire" McLeod, Hugh Matheson, Ronald Ross, Alexander Munro, Roderick McKenzie, Norman McLeod—seven boats in all. There would be no more until next summer.

In the clear colours of spring the harbour seemed even more beautiful than the explorers had remembered it. The men displayed it proudly to their families and took them to the sites of their homes. The walls of the little cabins which they had left waiting were still secure. Quickly they cut poles on which they laid layers of thick bark to form roofs, working with new assurance after their winter of hewing and building. Then in the tiny spaces which they had cleared on their former visit, they planted, among the stumps, the potatoes for next winter's use. Meanwhile there was abundant fish in the harbour; they would soon find sweet wild strawberries among the tall grass, and on open hillsides the low bushes now coming into leaf would presently bear rich clusters of blueberries.

About eight miles from its entrance the harbour of St. Ann's divides into two arms. The southern arm continues inland nearly three miles further, and by a small promontory is subdivided into two narrow bays known as North and South Guts. The promontory would be the centre of the settlement, a natural location for Norman McLeod. To its four hundred acres he laid claim, and to an area inland and adjoining it which would give to him an estate of more than 1,200 acres, nearly two square miles. Now he began to assume in fact the position he had won in spirit. He was chief. They gathered around him: south of South Gut, Norman McDonald, Squire McLeod, and Hugh Matheson; north of North Gut, Ronald Ross, Roderick McKenzie, and the Munro brothers at a little cape which soon was known as Munro's Point. Most of them would make the usual petition for two hundred acres of land.

Except for the huts at the harbour entrance there was no life at St. Ann's Bay, but in the soil that the new settlers' spades were breaking was the record of two centuries of settlement. In the summer of 1629, a French captain, Charles Daniel of Dieppe, was on his way to Quebec. Caught by a violent storm, his ship found shelter in the harbour. He intended to continue at once toward Quebec, but friendly Indians came to the shore with news of other ships entering the St. Lawrence. These, he knew, must be English. Prudently, he decided to stay.

Behind a high rock, still known as the Lookout, on the south side of the harbour entrance, he built barracks and a magazine and armed his new fort with eight pieces of cannon. He also provided a chapel for his companion, a Jesuit priest, Bartholomew Vipont.

In the week of Captain Daniel's arrival, a second French ship, also bound for Quebec, was wrecked on the rocks of Canso at the other end of the island. Saved from the wreck were two Jesuit fathers, Father Lallemant, the Superior of the Canadian Missions, who returned to France, and Father de Vieuxpont who was taken by Indians to Captain Daniel's fort. There, with Father Vipont, he began a mission to the Indians. They named the place and their chapel, Ste. Anne, probably because of a recommendation of Queen Anne of Austria, mother of Louis XIV.

After a year at St. Ann's, the two priests returned to France, but in the years after, other Jesuits came, including the revered Father Antoine Daniel, brother of the fort's founder, later martyred by the Iroquois at St. Joseph. Seven priests, in all, shared in this first Jesuit mission in Cape Breton. In the fort a garrison of about forty men was maintained, and around the fort, under its protection, settlers were encouraged to farm. To the harbour came French ships to trade with the Indians and to dry their fish.

After the mission was abandoned in 1641 most of the settlers left, but Simon Denys who had both a farm and a fishery remained for at least twenty years. His brother, the famous Nicholas Denys of St. Peter's, one-time governor of all this territory for the king of France, surveyed St. Ann's harbour and enthusiastically reported its possibilities—a harbour where vessels of three or four hundred tons could enter at all tides, where a thousand vessels could lie at anchor, protected by its narrow entrance, and so free of dangerous rocks that ships entering it could safely come so close to the land that the spar of the bowsprit could touch the cliff. He told of salmon and abundant mackerel in the harbour, shellfish on the sand bar, and, among the surrounding hills, ponds with good hunting for wild ducks, geese and other game.

For many years after Simon Denys had gone there was no life at the bay. The wild ducks settled fearlessly on the little lakes, and the balsams grew again on the abandoned farms. Sometimes there were fishermen who found a shelter in the bay, or landed to dry their catch on its sandy shore, but by official France, St. Ann's was forgotten.

Then, in 1713, came the end of Queen Anne's War and the treaty which gave Nova Scotia and Newfoundland to England, and left to the French Cape Breton and Prince Edward Island. For France, Cape Breton became the vital Atlantic possession, the guardian of her inland empire. At once officers were sent to appraise the site for a naval base which must be the greatest in North America.

Among them was Denys de la Ronde, grandson of Simon Denys. For him there was excitement in coming to the place which he had known from family tradition, in picking apples from the trees which his grandfather had planted. Extravagantly he reported that it was the most beautiful harbour in the world, a hundred thousand times finer than Havre a l'Anglais (Louisbourg), and able to be made impregnable at one-tenth of the cost. Other officers, too, urged the choice of St. Ann's, all ignoring the fact that its beautiful harbour was frozen over for three or four months each year.

On their recommendation, Fort Dauphin was built on the site of Captain Daniel's fort. Soldiers were brought in to work on the fortifications. In the harbour they built ships including one large enough to carry thirty-six pieces of cannon. Traders found it worthwhile to bring their wares from France. For six years the place bustled with activity. Then the French government made its final decision, choosing Louisbourg as the capital and sending brick and stone and skilled engineers to make it a great European stronghold.

To Louisbourg now went the great ships of the French fleet and the merchants and traders who had once visited little Fort Dauphin. At the fort only a small garrison remained. There were fishing stations, and some of the little farms were cultivated again. They sent provisions and quantities of firewood to supply the proud fortress of Louisbourg, but they lived undisturbed through the rise and fall of its fortunes, and, after its final capture, Fort Dauphin passed quietly to the English in 1760. When Norman and his companions came, the French had long since disappeared. There remained only the name of Cape Dauphin and the daffodils among the ruins of the fort.

Although there had been little farming at St. Ann's, another man, a century before Norman's arrival, had established a rural kingdom nearby. The Chevalier de la Boularderie had been granted the large island which lies just south of Cape Dauphin, almost barring the entrance to the Bras d'Or lake. This long, narrow island, nearly 100,000 acres in area, he named Boularderie, and on it he and his family lived for nearly thirty years. In their letters home to France they described their handsome buildings, including even a dairy and a dovecote, wind and water mills, and boasted of the fine wheat and vegetables which their land produced. The gracious establishment of the Chevalier with his twenty-five employees was deserted before Captain Holland came to survey the island for the British, but he, too, reported that Monsieur Boularderie's fine farm had produced grain equal to any in Canada.

In a few years even the last stragglers from the French settlements had vanished. By 1774, not one European of the total Cape Breton population lived in the large northern section which later became Victoria County. At Arichat and St. Peter's Bay at the other end of the island were the principal settlements—Acadian communities which made their living from fishing.

Probably about 1787, six or seven families came to St. Ann's, some by way of Sydney, others directly in fishing vessels. They were chiefly English, but there was one Irish family and a solitary American. This man, a bachelor from Virginia, a few years later hanged himself—the only violent act reported from St. Ann's since a brutal murder had shocked the French in the second year of their settlement.

But against the creatures of the forest there was an orgy of violence. It was now that the hunters came, from Newfoundland and the settlements in Nova Scotia and Prince Edward Island, to kill the moose which roamed in thousands through the northern part of the island. In the late winter when the moose crashed heavily through the crusted snow it was easy for hunters on snowshoes to run them down. Their meat was the mainstay of the few settlers, but the visiting hunters tossed it aside except for what they could eat on the spot. Sometimes they kept the nose of the moose, called *moufle*, which was made into soup and considered a great delicacy. Their prize was the skin. For the skins they got ten shillings each, and for them they slaughtered the moose in droves, 9,000 in the winter of 1789 alone. The following year troops moved in and put a stop to the carnage.

None of the hunters stayed at St. Ann's. A few years later a German family named Willhausen came by way of the Nova Scotia mainland. Their name remained in Willhausen Point on the southern shore of the bay. From that time until the coming of the Scottish settlers, the settlement received no additions from outside. Fishing vessels came into the harbour, and a man from the Jersey Islands had a fishing station at what is known as Ramo's Beach, presumably named after him.

In 1820, only a tiny handful of settlers on the south shore of the bay remained from nearly two centuries of life at St. Ann's. The Scots who had newly come were from the Old Land, but this place which to them seemed empty and new had long ago been touched by an Old World culture more advanced than anything that they had known. It had not survived. Now the new settlers must find in their harsher background the qualities which would enable them not only to survive but to prosper.

In the year of their arrival, Cape Breton, a separate province since 1784, was reunited to Nova Scotia. Its history since the conquest had been marked by confusion and indecision. During the first years no land was granted on the island. Then, after 1784, it was given a separate government under Lieutenant-Governor Des Barres, and Loyalists from the American colonies were invited to apply for land. A group of them founded the town of Sydney. Few others came; only scattered individuals who settled near Sydney or Baddeck, or by the Strait of Canso. Although the hope of a Loyalist island had faded, the separate administration continued until 1820 when it became so involved in internal disputes that its duties were taken over by the government of the mainland.

So it was to Halifax that Norman sent at the end of the year his petition for the lot on which he was settled "at the head of the harbour of St. Ann's or Port Dauphine, 300 or 400 acres." The recommendation was signed by Rev. H. Binney, Rector of the parish of Sydney and by Leonard, Clarke and Bown, Justices of the Peace. They wrote from Sydney, December 20, 1820: "Mr. Norman McCloud who is now Petitioning for land at St. Ann's appearing to us to be a very respectable seriously disposed person who had received a classical education, we beg humbly to recommend him as worthy of any encouragement which his Excellency the Lieutenant Governor may be pleased to afford."[1]

[1] Cape Breton Land Papers, no. 2742.

In Scotland, on the *Frances Ann*, at Pictou, the people about him had learned to rely on Norman's spiritual strength. They were willing that he should take for them the tremendous responsibility which he claimed. Now as he petitioned first for a large block of land, with the special approval of the Sydney authorities, he was starting toward the official recognition of his leadership which had to come before he could guide and protect his chosen people as his conscience and ambition demanded. To be effectively spiritual his rule must also be temporal and he had taken the first step toward its establishment on the historic shores of St. Ann's.

CHAPTER SEVEN

With Lawful Authority

IN THE FIRST DAYS of the new settlement, the little circle of friends whose farms surrounded Norman accepted his leadership without question. In considering him as their minister they would naturally cede to him the wide authority held by their parish clergyman at home. Each man, too, had personal reasons for allowing his domineering friend to direct his life.

With the Munro brothers, their youth was probably an important factor. In 1820, Alexander Munro was thirty years old. He was a graduate of King's College, Aberdeen, and had been a teacher in Scotland before he accepted Norman's invitation to emigrate to Pictou. He came not only with education, but with the capital which had enabled him to be the chief financier of the *Ark*, and to buy her outright from the other shareholders after their arrival at St. Ann's. With the confident assurance characteristic of his family he immediately registered not only his requirement for land at St. Ann's, but also the name of his estate, "Ballach Laddich."

Such a man would seem unlikely to have freely accepted anyone's leadership. But it was not long since he had been an impressionable youth in their home in Assynt when Norman was fighting his way through to spiritual certainty and becoming the wonder of the community. He could understand better than most of Norman's contemporaries the intellectual side of his struggle. Strong and progressive though he was, Alexander Munro was not himself a leader. It was not strange, then, that he should still look with respect to the man, ten years his senior, who richly possessed the personal magnetism which was his own great lack. It was also inevitable that with the passage of years there would be a widening rift between them.

Alexander's younger brother, Donald, a competent man of twenty-five who settled beside him at Munro's Point, quietly took his part in the building of the new settlement. John, the youngest Munro, was a precocious lad who had arrived in Pictou at the age of seventeen and had immediately opened a school at Cariboo. Two years later, he was becoming a landowner at St. Ann's and was registering his new estate under the name of "Klas More." In the summers he went to work in the fisheries at Cape North; within five years he acquired other lots along the shore, and in 1825 he entered into a business partnership which would soon establish him as the commercial leader of St. Ann's. In these early years, the arrogance which was later said to distinguish "the mighty Munro" was only a boy's confident enthusiasm. It would be many years before it would challenge the rule of Norman McLeod.

Alexander Munro's young wife who kept house for her husband and his bachelor brothers shared the loneliness of the first settlement with her older sister, Jane, the wife of Norman McDonald who lived across the bay with her lively young family. McDonald, a contemporary of Norman McLeod, was a far-sighted intelligent man whose children had already reached an age when their schooling and their future opportunities were a keen concern. It was so, too, with Ronald Ross and Roderick McKenzie. Their experience on the rocky little farms in Assynt had given them no reason to think of farming as a satisfying or rewarding career for an intelligent man. As well as by their personal friendship for Norman McLeod and their adherence to his religious principles they were held by the assurance that with him there would be an orderly community in which to bring up their families, and a school and church, still lacking in many new world settlements, to prepare them for a fuller and more profitable life.

Squire Donald McLeod was one member of the pioneer group at St. Ann's whose devotion to Norman was preeminently spiritual. He was older than Norman, and at their home in Assynt had watched the struggles and triumphs of the fierce young man. He joined him in deploring the practices and the preachers of the Established Church. Behind the practical common sense which guided his business affairs, Donald McLeod had a mystic strain which responded to the intensity of Norman's spirit. He truly felt that his minister was divinely inspired.

Though he was a gentle man who would be glad to see people content in this world as well as in the next, he accepted as a necessary accompaniment of his divine calling the harshness which accompanied Norman's fearless certainty. In return, Norman could afford to show to him, an older man, the milder and gentler side of his nature. For a time the Squire shared in the leadership of the settlement. Finally an act of the Squire's kindly good will would bring them into bitter conflict.

Although many others would soon join them, these first settlers would continue to be the strong men of the settlement. Their situation was difficult and their homes rude, but they had not come ill-equipped from Scotland. For the Sunday service at Norman's rough log cabin they wore their black frock coats. It was a strange solemn sight in the wilderness—a symbol of the personal dignity with which each man approached his God, a dignity which would eventually bring each of them into some degree of conflict with God's representative among them.

The isolation into which they settled that winter after the ice had closed the harbour was more complete than anyone in the little settlement had ever known. Their soil had produced a good crop of potatoes, and these, with fish, usually boiled together in a pot over the fire, saw them through the winter. For special occasions there were the reserves of meal that they had brought from Pictou. For other supplies, the only store nearer than Sydney, forty miles away, was a little shop kept by James Duffus on the island at Baddeck. There was yet no blazed trail to Baddeck and even in summer the trip took a whole day. In winter storms with no place to take shelter on the way it was perilous for men unaccustomed to the woods.

For the novice axemen even the cutting of wood for the fire was a heavy task. Although the chinks between the round spruce logs of the cabins were filled with moss, the wind still found its way through and frost coated the inside walls. The green logs of this first winter often smouldered sluggishly, but to keep the fire blazing in the stone fireplace was the only defence against the cold. Day and night they watched it and kept it going.

For some of the children that winter the fire had to take the place of warm clothing. When their clothes and shoes were outgrown and worn out there were few replacements, sometimes not even patches nor the needle and thread for sewing them on. There was little wool to be spun into the material for new clothing, and for shoes only the chance killing of a moose or deer could provide the hides. Close by the fire in the little cabins, the children waited for the passing of winter.

Even those who could safely be out of doors felt the isolation of that winter. Their homes, on the waterfront of their 200-acre farms, were relatively close to their neighbours by boat. But they feared the dark forest without a sign of road or trail. Not without reason. From Pictou they knew the terrible stories of being lost in the woods, of wandering in blizzards, and perishing blindly a few yards from shelter. In midwinter when the harbour ice was solid they could safely cross on foot. The dangerous time was in early winter when the newly-formed ice blocked the bay but would not carry a man's weight, and in early spring just before the break-up.

To the St. Ann's settlers, still inexperienced in the woods, the greatest boon that first winter was a little group of young men who had come early in the autumn to North River, a few miles along the shore. Among them were two brothers, John and Peter Fraser who, unlike the other settlers, were natives of Pictou. They were descendants of one of the Fraser Highlanders who took part in the capture of Quebec and was later granted land in Nova Scotia. They had grown up in the woods, they knew the ways of the weather, and they had been hunters since their childhood. Inevitably, as their nearest neighbours, they would have offered practical help to the people of St. Ann's. They were particularly generous since John Fraser was already making regular trips across the harbour to see the Squire's daughter, Mary, whom he later married. The little group at North River was soon closely connected with the St. Ann's community, and when, in the following year, some of Norman's old friends from Assynt joined them they were firmly attached to his congregation.

The years of the first settlement at St. Ann's would see a great influx of Highlanders even into the remote parts of Cape Breton. There had been a steady trickle of immigration since the time, eighteen years before, when the first shipload of Highland immigrants had arrived in Sydney. These people and many of their poverty-stricken successors were desperately in need of the help which the little town of Sydney generously gave. Most of them remained for a time in the Sydney district, but by 1820 the newcomers and even some who had lived there for a few years were beginning to scatter throughout the island. Baddeck, Middle River, Grand Narrows, Ingonish, Boularderie—all would have new settlers from Scotland in the first years of the 1820s.

The Highlanders from the Scottish coasts and islands, fishermen and seafarers, were particularly attracted to Cape Breton which closely resembled their homes. By the 1820s, although many were still coming as refugees from the poverty and uncertainty of the Highlands, there were other enterprising men who followed their countrymen, not as confused immigrants but as purposeful men of business. In combination the two types could create strong self-contained communities.

To the men from the rocky inlets of the coast of Assynt, the wide landlocked harbour of St. Ann's, without rock or shoal for six miles, sounded like an impossible dream come true. As Alex Munro's *Ark* sailed back and forth to Pictou bringing supplies and livestock for the new settlers, the stories of the wonderful harbour with its teeming fish and its empty shore quickly circulated among Norman's friends who were inland settlers at Pictou. They were sure of his strength and guidance, they were uneasily aware of his warnings about the wickedness of Pictou, and they needed the sea. Pictou, with its pioneer agricultural society and its fertile land, was beginning to be a centre of progressive farming, but they had for generations been accustomed to fishing and farming in combination, with the farm as their base of operations but fishing as their hope of increased income and of progress. They were not willing to trust themselves completely to the tree-covered land. Security was in their old resource, the sea.

Many of Norman's friends from Pictou followed to St. Ann's the next spring. At almost the same time another shipload of Highland immigrants arrived in Pictou. These, too, made their way to St. Ann's. Among them was a bevy of McLeods, many of them distantly related to Norman, with such a formidable array of similar names that they were identified by the Gaelic equivalents of "Big," "Old," "Red," and "Black." Direct from Scotland, too, new settlers came, some by way of Sydney, some dropped at St. Ann's by ships on their way to Pictou. By the end of 1821 the ring of settlement had tightened around the harbour. Within ten years, St. Ann's would be a thickly settled community.

On his large block of land at the head of the harbour, Norman had a central position in the fast-growing settlement. His spiritual leadership was unlikely to face any immediate challenge from within. Most of the new settlers sorely needed strength and direction. For it they were accustomed to look to their minister. His experience in Scotland had shown him, however, that spiritual leadership could be severely handicapped from without by government and the law. He was confident that he knew God's will for the people, but his hope of translating a doctrine into a way of life depended on an all-inclusive leadership. He could achieve it only if there were no rival leaders in other spheres.

Potentially there was such a leader at Baddeck. James Duffus was a gay young half-pay naval officer who had come there two years before and opened a small store on the Duke of Kent's Island. Its location was central for the people in the little settlements around the Bras d'Or lakes. Customers without boats found their way through the woods to the shore, signalled to the island and were fetched and returned by canoe. Duffus may have lacked the long vision of his brother-in-law, Samuel Cunard, but he had a lively imagination. Credulous Highlanders watched him spellbound as he described how he got the long scar across his forehead. It was in the fight between the *Shannon* and the *Chesapeake*, he said, and dramatically he went through the battle, thrusting and parrying gloriously until the captain of the *Chesapeake* slashed his forehead and he, with a mighty blow, cut off the captain's head and left him kicking on the deck. That Duffus was an officer on the *Falcon* and that Captain Lawrence of the *Chesapeake* had been killed by a musket ball did not hurt the story a particle.

His business throve. He had a boat which made regular journeys to Halifax; in 1820 he was appointed magistrate. This appointment, among other duties, gave him the right to perform marriages in the district immediately surrounding Baddeck. Since there was no one else with authority to marry he presently went beyond his limits and married a few couples from St. Ann's and Middle River. The clergy considered these ceremonies inadequate. A minister later refused to baptize the children of the Middle River couples until he had married them again.

In 1823, as soon as the population of the St. Ann's district warranted it, Norman secured his own appointment as magistrate. Now he represented the law for St. Ann's, temporal and spiritual. He still felt, however, that the maintaining of divine authority and the guarding of the people against the laxities and freedoms of the new land, demanded that marriage should be not a civil but a religious ceremony. This ceremony, since he had left the Church of Scotland unlicensed and unordained, he could not perform. To rectify the situation he set out for the United States in the summer of 1826, determined to return licensed and ordained as a minister.

Since the Church in the United States had no State connection it was free from the objection which had made the Church of Scotland unacceptable to him. Also on the distant shores of Cape Breton he could not in any practical sense be subject to rules or limitations set by a presbytery in the United States. He had been reassured on these points when in the winter of 1821 he had paid a short visit to Ohio. It may have been on that trip that he met Alexander Denoon, minister of a Presbyterian Church in Caledonia, N.Y., in the Geneva Presbytery of New York State. Now he asked Mr. Denoon to sponsor him through the period required for his acceptance into the Church.

Although undoubtedly they would be known to each other

as dissenters against the Established Church, it does not seem likely that they were personally acquainted in Scotland. Their histories were similar. Denoon, a native of Campbeltown, Argyllshire, had studied classics and theology at the University of Aberdeen. He had been for twelve years a parochial teacher, part of the time at Inverness in the parish from which many of the Caledonia settlers had emigrated. Like Norman at Lochbroom he had lectured in the church on the Sundays when the minister was absent. Since he refused to become a minister in the Church of Scotland under the domination of the State, the Caledonia immigrants invited him to come to the United States as their minister. He arrived in 1806, and, despite opposition from a faction of the Caledonia Church, he was ordained two years later.

The dissension continued, however; the congregation divided and for most of the twenty years before Norman's coming, he and his group had been meeting in one of the members' houses. The other faction, after arguments, lawsuits and even fist fights, held the log church. Such a situation Norman would never have tolerated. Mr. Denoon was of a different stamp, his stout, short figure contrasting sharply with the lean intensity of Norman. The curled auburn wig which hung against his shoulders was a pretty thing beside the straight black hair that flapped to Norman's vigorous words. In Denoon's speech were still the mystical elements which had previously caused the practical members of his congregation to accuse him of preaching error and nonsense.

Norman's year with Mr. Denoon is not mentioned in the official history of the Caledonia congregation, but perhaps it is significant that it was in that year that Mr. Denoon and his congregation finally built their new stone church.

Mr. Denoon introduced him to the presbytery and Norman produced testimonials of "his church membership, moral character and attention to literary pursuits." Satisfied by his references, the presbytery agreed to examine him two weeks later. On that occasion he exhibited a written lecture on a legalistic passage from St. Paul's "Epistle to the Romans," and a popular discourse as part of his trials for licence. It was unanimously agreed that he be licensed to preach within the Geneva presbytery or "wherever else he shall be orderly called."

With Mr. Denoon in the village of Caledonia Norman spent the winter. The village and its surrounding township were slightly more than twenty-five years old. The little village was composed of the usual grist mill, sawmill and fulling mill, stores and taverns. Most of the houses clustered around them were of sawn lumber, and close to the main corner was Major Gad Blakslee's new stone house. The farm lands showed the hard work and careful planning which had quickly built a thriving community. The census indicates their prosperity—247 horses were owned among the 194 electors! At St. Ann's there was not yet a horse nor use for one. Neither at this time nor later, however, is there any sign that Norman might still wish to remove himself or his people to this more highly developed country. Perhaps the answers are in the fact that all the people of Caledonia had been enthusiastic supporters of the United States in the recent war of 1812, and in Norman's comment, many years later, on the arrogance of the Americans in defence of their independence.

The next July at a special session in Caledonia the presbytery received Norman's request for ordination. After hearing him preach another sermon and receiving a resolution that "the people among whom he has laboured for ten months past express the most entire confidence in his piety and usefulness," presbytery acceded to his request and he was ordained a minister of the Presbyterian Church.

Immediately he set out for home, by the new Erie Canal and the Hudson River. Now, though his authority in the log church which they had built at St. Ann's in 1822 could not possibly be increased, he had in addition the legal rights to perform the ceremonies and dispense the sacraments of the Church. He explained to a Scottish friend many years later, in telling the circumstances of his ordination: "My privilege on this ground is singular. Being placed at a distance I have never experienced the least restraint or control.... Otherwise I would not have thought of joining any clergy for all my life in the world."

His position as minister at St. Ann's was legally unassailable. Only one sphere of community life was yet to be controlled. The school which he had opened in 1822 under his own tuition must be officially recognized by the government of Nova Scotia. Before the end of 1827 he would have completed the necessary steps toward obtaining a licence as schoolmaster for Norman McLeod, Esquire, of St. Ann's.

CHAPTER EIGHT

Cape Breton Schoolmaster

WHEN NORMAN began classes in his home in the summer of 1822 he became one of the pioneers in Cape Breton education. Even in Sydney the progress of the elementary school had been slow and contentious. In that year the first grammar school was opening there with eleven pupils of whom ten were Latin scholars.

After the reunion of Cape Breton and Nova Scotia, the Lieutenant-Governor had appointed a commission to investigate education in Cape Breton. In 1824 they reported that in the entire island there were only five common schools—"at Sydney, Arichat, Margaree, Baddeck and Banackady," with an average attendance of about twenty pupils. There were various arrangements with the teachers. At Baddeck the master received forty pounds, half in cash and half in produce; at Margaree five families employed the master for twenty pounds, chiefly in produce, and lodged him from house to house. The tuition allowance was usually about ten shillings per quarter for each child, and the commissioners estimated that in many places about one-quarter of the parents would not be able to pay anything toward their children's education.

It would seem that at this time Norman's classes, conducted at his home or in the church building, were not sufficiently regular to be classed as a school. St. Ann's is listed among the eight places "in which from poverty of the inhabitants no schools are yet established and in which they are really needed." An individual report by one of the commissioners mentions it as a place in which "travelling teachers are occasionally employed." St. Ann's must already have been a large settlement and its people enthusiastic for education, since the commissioners recommended that if the money available for grants could be divided among only six schools, one of them should be St. Ann's.

Provincial grants and other aspects of provincial assistance and control were just beginning to have a part in school planning. Throughout Nova Scotia, including Cape Breton, a series of Education Acts by 1826 established the pattern which elementary schools would follow for the first half of the century. The Justices of the Peace were authorized to divide the inhabited parts of the province into school districts small enough that a schoolhouse would be reasonably near the pupils' homes. When two-thirds of the rateable inhabitants of a school district had certified their desire for a school the district was to choose three trustees for the approval of the Justices of the Peace. The trustees were to manage the school property, employ licensed teachers and report regularly on enrolment, attendance and expenditures to the Board of Commissioners of their county or district, who in turn were appointed by the Lieutenant-Governor. The commissioners were to superintend and inspect the schools, license teachers, establish regulations and a course of instruction, and report to the legislature. If possible the teacher was to be paid a minimum of fifty pounds, part of which might be paid in kind. Trustees might hire for less if they could, but they would be penalized ten pounds for hiring an unlicensed teacher. The costs were to be raised by an equal rate of assessment or by subscription. For many years to come, however, schools were financed by subscription. The people, generally, were too proud to allow others to pay by assessment for the education of their children. It was understood that if fifty pounds was raised locally for the support of a school, the trustees would receive a grant of twenty-five pounds from the provincial government, and a like proportion for any sum not exceeding two hundred pounds. Throughout the years the provincial grants fluctuated, and there were periodic changes in regulations, but basically the pattern remained constant until mid-century.

By the terms of this act Cape Breton was regarded as one district with two hundred and twenty pounds at its disposal. Its commissioners, Charles Inglis, John G. Marshall and Thomas

Crawley, divided it into fifty-one districts, but schools did not immediately appear. Their report for 1827 shows that only six are in operation, but it also states that they have granted licences as schoolmasters to seven persons including Norman McLeod, Esq. of St. Ann's. They report that "for the School districts of St. Ann's and Little Baddeck, subscriptions have been completed, schools established, and a time and place appointed by the magistrates for the Inhabitants to choose trustees." "Assessment," they proudly conclude, "has in no case been resorted to."

Although progress was slow at first, the Commission agreed with everyone who has written of Cape Breton in these early years that the people were eager for education and anxious to obtain schools. It seems that in the beginning they moved slowly because they failed to understand the benefits of the act. Grants of money from the State, based on their own contributions and initiative, differed from the custom of their homeland. There the schools had been associated with the Church and under its control. The school building was maintained by the Church which also paid the schoolmaster a basic salary to be augmented by the fees of the students. Now they were free from the Established Church and from the control of the landlord, but with freedom they had acquired the responsibilities which churches and landlords had formerly borne. In education they were quick to assume their new responsibility—in less than twenty-five years the six schools of 1827 had increased to 179.

Their enthusiasm might seem remarkable since not one-fifth of the heads of families could read or write, but the low rate of literacy was no indication of their intelligence. Since many of them had been fully grown before Gaelic schools were established in their home parishes in Scotland, they had had no opportunity to read or write the only language they knew. Only the men and women under the age of thirty to whom Gaelic schools had been available were uniformly literate.

To people who had been deprived by circumstances of the education for which they were often abundantly equipped it was desperately important that their children should learn to read. Also, as the population was rapidly increasing, it was evident that the land, even when it was supplemented by the fisheries, would not comfortably support them all. Many of them knew little of towns, but even in Pictou they had seen how a New World town could grow. They heard of little places in the United States which had grown in one man's lifetime into busy ports or thriving commercial centres. Such towns would need educated men. To these Highlanders, fully aware of their dignity and equality, it seemed a proud but not impossible thing that these men should be their sons.

Although the future was full of promise, the present was very drab in the little schools of Cape Breton. At one end of the schoolroom stood the platform with the teacher's desk, at the other, the big stone fireplace. Long benches running the length of the room served as seats, and often the student's knee was his only desk. The schools had no equipment. It would be many years before there were prescribed textbooks; at this time it was very hard to get any kind of book. From whatever was available, however ill suited to their age or comprehension, the children read. Among these handicaps there could be only two positive factors—the parents' enthusiasm for their children's education, and the quality of the teacher. In both of these points the children of St. Ann's were fortunate.

That Norman McLeod, teacher of School District 20, south side St. Ann's, and Alexander Munro, School District 19, north side St. Ann's, were unusually intelligent men who had had a thorough formal education marked them out among the early teachers. Many years later when J. W. Dawson, the newly appointed Superintendent of Schools, made his tour of inspection, he found that the teachers often knew very little of the subjects they professed to teach. "Lessons in reading without any explanation or mental training, columns of unintelligible spellings, inability to explain the principles of arithmetic or the elements of English grammar, or to preserve order except by the harshest and most repulsive methods formed the rule rather than the exception."[1]

These conditions were almost inevitable since there was no

[1] Harvey, D. C., "Origin of our Normal Schools," *Journal of Education*, p. 566, September 1937.

way of imposing any standard upon the teachers. The main requirement for obtaining a licence from the Commission was the recommendation of a clergyman, and, when no better person was available, he was sometimes compelled to approve a mediocre man or one who, while possessing the requisite knowledge, was temperamentally unsuited to teaching.

Report and tradition agree that Norman was an excellent teacher. Alone of all his endeavours his school seems usually to have satisfied everyone—the provincial authorities, the parents and the pupils. Although he was equally fluent in both languages, he taught the common school in Gaelic. The students began with the alphabet, then progressed to the "little Spelling book" and the "larger Spelling book." The New Testament was the next textbook, followed by the complete Bible, and then by English reading and writing. Writing and arithmetic came only in the later years of the common school curriculum, perhaps because of the scarcity of slates. In a pioneer school where distance, weather and farm work could all interfere with school attendance, age groups meant nothing. An annual report shows that one twelve-year-old has just completed the alphabet and is beginning the spelling book, another of the same age has completed the Bible and is beginning English reading and writing, and a thirteen-year-old boy who has spent the past term translating the English New Testament into Gaelic is now about to begin the translation of the Old Testament.

By boat across the harbour or scuffling along the crooked trails through the woods, sixty-nine children came in the autumn of 1829 to Norman's school at the head of the harbour. There were big boys like Norman's own sixteen-year-old son John and his friend John Ross. Little Mary Fraser was only five, but since she lived very close to the school she tagged along on fine days with her older brother and sister. There never was a minimum age of starting school. Two years later Norman's own Peggy, her father's pet and the darling of the whole settlement, started to his school at the age of three.

Only Norman's six children and the Squire's family had a perfect record of attendance, six days a week, through the autumn term of 1829. There were many summer chores—picking berries, herding cattle, minding younger brothers and sisters. For the older boys there was farm work and fishing to cut into their school time in summer. A partial summer attendance was a regularly accepted thing. Still it must have been irksome to bright students to see the minister's family, who were allowed to attend regularly, held up as examples of progress. Particularly when one reason for other pupils missing school was that their fathers were working away from home on Norman's farm to pay their school subscriptions.

Norman accepted payment of subscriptions in labour only. To be paid in money or even in produce would have made him in part the people's servant; to be paid in labour left him still the master. Theoretically he was hired as a teacher, and in his report for December 1st, 1829, he describes the arrangements: "The school is supported by subscription. The amount raised is forty pounds for Teacher, fourteen pounds for schoolhouse. The teacher's salary is at the rate of sixty pounds per annum. The allowance for board, lodging and washing is at the rate of ten shillings per week." In some districts the teacher's allowance for board, lodging and washing was provided by having him live each week at the house of one pupil. To Norman, it, like the forty pounds of salary, was paid in labour on his farm. Twenty-eight men, in that year of 1829, would give to the clearing and cultivating of Norman's farm many hours of hard labour in return for their children's education. It was no token payment, Norman knew what was to be done and saw to it that it was done well. In addition he received in cash the provincial grant of twenty pounds.

Alexander Munro kept a smaller school at the north side of the harbour, with an enrolment that year of thirty-seven pupils. The subscriptions at his school were usually paid in equal amounts of cash and produce, and his brothers' families made their complete payment in cash.

The trustees in Norman's district were Squire McLeod, John Munro and Roderick Fraser. These appointments, based on the nomination of the community, were finally made by the Commission in Sydney, and changes were made only at the pleasure of the Commission. Teachers sometimes intervened or found it their duty to inform the Commission about their trustees. One of the neighbouring teachers wrote to the Sydney office about his trustees: "James Guinn is the best Schollar [*sic*] and best judge of a school that I find in this place, yet I have it against him that he makes it a point of necessity to set his nets on Sabbath evening. His continuation in the Trusteeship solely depends on you." In later years, Norman, too, would carry tales to the Commission.

Attendance at Norman's school continually increased until in the second half of 1831 it reached its peak of 110 pupils. By this time, in addition to Alexander Munro's school, there were two other schools reporting from St. Ann's—from the southeastern and northeastern districts. In all, 210 students were attending school at St. Ann's in the autumn of 1831. In the following year there is a sharp slump in enrolment at Norman's school. From 110 it dropped to 38. Even from Norman's family the younger and the older children are missing, and the same pattern holds in the other families. There are two probable reasons. 1832 was the first year of serious crop failure and famine, small children may have had to be kept at home for lack of food and clothing. Probably, too, the older children had completed their common school education. This latter seems likely since in 1835 the enrolment had risen again to 84 with 30 of the children "instructed under the regulation of Grammar School." In that year all of Norman's nine children were back at school from John, aged twenty-one, to little five-year-old Edward, and the teacher's salary, with a new provincial grant to the combined school, and more labour from the community, had risen to one hundred and twenty pounds a year.

Concurrent with the development of the Cape Breton schools under government direction was a missionary impulse from Scotland. In 1825 the Glasgow Colonial Missionary Society had been formed to aid Scottish colonists in North America by sending out or assisting to send out ministers, catechists and schoolteachers. Two years after its formation it sent two Nova Scotia ministers to tour Cape Breton and study conditions there. Their report of the poverty of the people and the tremendous need for ministers and teachers stirred the imagination of a young Scottish woman, Mrs. Isabella Gordon Mackay. Immediately she founded the Edinburgh Ladies' Association whose sole object was to help the people of Cape Breton.

Mrs. Mackay was an energetic woman with boundless enthusiasm and genuine devotion to her cause. Her enthusiasm was so infectious that under her leadership the Association sent out eight ministers as well as catechists and teachers. The ladies not only contributed to their salaries but provided hundreds of Bibles and school books. Mrs. Mackay corresponded directly and constantly with every one of her ministers and teachers so that each immediate need was answered—special requests for books, for bed clothing, for hemp to be spun into fishing nets when the crops had failed. Her whole life centred in her Association. After her husband's death she even disposed of her comfortable estate and boarded in a friend's home in order to give every possible shilling to her missions. In her single-minded enthusiasm for her good cause, she seems to have centred in herself the whole direction of her project and ignored the building of a strong organization at home. Within a year of her death the society had disbanded. But in its time it had made an outstanding contribution to Cape Breton life of the second quarter-century.

In her strong aggressive personality she was almost a female counterpart of Norman McLeod. Inevitably she fell foul of him. He claimed that her missionaries were misrepresenting conditions on the island in order to magnify the results and the necessity of their own labours, that they contributed nothing to the improvement of the land, and that some of their followers sold the articles which had been sent out for the poor. Probably these matters were among the complaints which he listed in his letters to her. The replies showed her, he said, to be "impolite, insolent and vicious." And as for the missions to which she gave all her resources and energy—"That silly and selfish lady cares no more for the care of souls than Jehu for the worship of God, but only while her religious zeal and service seem to enhance her credit among her purblind and self-interested dependents and adherents in order to feed her most manifest and dominant pride."[2]

[2] McLeod, Norman, op. cit., p. 134.

Did he ever think that the same comment might have been applied to his own work? Or was it because he was aware of the same weaknesses in himself that he could stab unerringly at the human faults latent in even the greatest undertakings? He claimed to distinguish between speaking evil of men and speaking necessarily of their evil. It would seem, however, that he usually found it necessary to speak most loudly of the evil of those who were his rivals in leadership.

Norman's closest contact with the representatives of the Ladies' Association came when Mr. Alexander Munro and his wife arrived from Scotland in 1839 to open a school on Boularderie Island within twenty miles of St. Ann's. Munro (not to be confused with Alexander Munro who had come with Norman to St. Ann's and taught there) had been educated at Marischal College, Aberdeen, and at the Normal School in Glasgow. He was prepared not only to teach the necessary subjects, but also to train teachers. Norman's pupils also were being licensed as teachers. He now had another rival in Munro.

The Munros were the most serious rivals he had yet encountered. Since Mrs. Munro was also a qualified teacher, they were uniquely equipped to make their school a centre of rural Cape Breton. They had only one handicap, that their school was conducted entirely in English. By 1839, however, many of the families who were intensely interested in their children's education had acquired a passable knowledge of English.

Alexander Munro's first letter to the Edinburgh Association, December 25th, 1839, described his plans and his progress: "I soon found that there was neither schoolhouse nor dwelling house for me, so I am obliged to teach in the church and live in a log house far from comfortable, being smoky and the other end of it being occupied by a large young family. We commenced teaching on Nov. 21st and have 60 scholars. The whooping cough has kept many away. In a week or two I expect some pupils from St. Ann's, and two lads from Middle River have taken up their abode in a small hut beside the school. We are unable fully to carry out the training system, as we could wish, for want of a gallery. I have mounted the maps on rollers at my own expense and I suppose I shall have to put the pictures on boards also. I should have many more young men, had I a pair of globes. We open at half past nine and continue till dark about 4 o'clock with an interval of fifteen minutes." He also mentioned that he could have had a salary of two hundred pounds and Mrs. Munro eighty pounds by remaining as teachers in Halifax.

Letters from Mrs. Munro explained her way of teaching the girls whose families put up log huts for them so that they might live near the school. Sometimes their mothers came with them. "I have thirty girls sewing, from nine to twenty-four years of age and expect more through the winter. They are exceedingly bright and anxious to learn. Only two or three are tolerable sewers, but they all try to imitate my work and are succeeding astonishingly well, considering their apparatus. There is not a pair of scissors in the school but mine. Few of them can manage to bring more than one needle at a time. They depend on me for these supplies. I got some threads from a store, but they are of the most inferior quality at double price. The unbleached cotton is a double boon, first as work for the girls and then to be distributed among the most needful. The tippets I distributed on the 2nd day of the year. The mutches I have given to some and only wait to be acquainted with the old women's circumstances to dispose of the rest."

Later she wrote: "Our school is still on the increase, about 100 in all. I have forty girls sewing. There are five teachers training. We take in the evening the teachers and any scholars who choose to attend, without charging any additional fee. All who are near come. Mr. Munro teaches them grammar, arithmetic and any subject in which they are deficient. I teach them singing."

Around the Munros was developing a relaxed social atmosphere in sharp contrast to the austerity of Norman's school. In return, Norman sneered at Normal Schools and their products: "The space of a few months in one of these seminaries is far preferable to the tedious course of many years under any other system. A mere dolt and dullard, drilled there for a winter, will then spring forth and strut about, an adept in learning, in all the branches necessary for his intended station. Our neighbour Smerky is a notable instance on this ground; under the patronage of the Ladies' Association, though previously labouring under special disadvantages, yet having passed a short session in one of those schools at Glasgow, he is now perfectly capable of what not. He can calculate and tell you the courses, distances and dimensions of Jupiter, Uranus and Georgium Sidus; treat of the Equator, the Hemispheres, and the twelve signs of the Zodiac; and talk of monkeys and mummies, of the ruins of Babel and the pyramids of Egypt. 'A noun is a name, a verb is a word'; and so of all the rest of the parts of speech, which must prove a vast improvement in the wonderful training system! as also '4 times 5 is 20'; 'No! but 4 five times are equal to 20.' By the help of maps and shapes from Scotland which are pompously suspended in his schoolhouse Smerky can tell his pupils the disposition of a tiger by physiognomy.... To play properly with dogs and cats, and to exercise the mental powers and corporal faculties of these simple though useful animals; to swing and swingle, to joggle and dangle; and all this rare and exemplary amusement in the view, by the help and for the benefit and improvement of the mind and body of his scholars are, you must know, some of the indispensable duties and training of the normal teacher."[3]

It is the eternal complaint of the scholar against the technician. Norman later admitted that Normal Schools might have some merit but that they foolishly promised far beyond their power to perform, and tended to substitute method for matter in teaching. Was there, too, an element of envy in his sneer at maps and shapes from Scotland? He was proudly independent of the equipment which was essential to Mr. Munro, but he must have contrasted his own difficulties in obtaining books and supplies, with the abundant first, second, third, fourth and fifth books, priced from 2d. to 2s. 6d., recorded in the account books of the Munro school. Not for anything in the world would he have accepted the restraints imposed by the patronage of any association. Yet its benefits must have appeared somewhat attractive, particularly when he saw them bestowed on a teacher whom he considered so much less worthy than himself.

At the time of the Munros' coming Norman would be unu-

[3] ibid., p. 83.

sually aware of his position because, in his own school, his authority had recently been challenged. The punishments which he inflicted on his students were not unusually severe, since in the schools of the early nineteenth century, corporal punishment was the accepted rule. The parents expected it. There is more than one report of a father bringing his little boy to school and admonishing the teacher to be sure to whip him every day. The pupils consequently were prepared for rough treatment and the fact that most of them as adults spoke gratefully of Norman's kindness and his excellent teaching would not necessarily imply gentleness.

An unwritten rule was that, though other forms of punishment might be inflicted on girls, the birch rod was for boys only. There was a day when Norman, goaded to fury by an attractive young girl, reached for the birch rod. The pupils gasped. Isaac McLeod, the Squire's youngest son, looked up from his work. He bounded to the platform, and before the master could turn, his hand was on the rod. In a moment, quiet, orderly Isaac had the stick in both his hands and he and the master were pulling each other across the room in a crazy tug-of-war. The girl stood for a minute, rooted to the spot, then she darted for the door and with one horrified glance over her shoulder, raced away through the woods. Norman was immensely strong, but young Isaac was lithe and lightning quick. All his years of silent protest were in this moment. With a sudden twist the rod was in his hands. He sprang for the door, then, secure on the threshold, flung the rod contemptuously aside and strode from the school. Neither Isaac nor any of the Squire's family ever returned.

The records of the Munros' school, called the Boularderie Academy, show on December 18th, 1839, the registration of Isaac McLeod, son of Donald McLeod Esq. The next month's records show that he bought one fifth book for 2s. 6d. The records of July, 1841, list a "large map, 2 small Europ. Pol. and 7 bxes Jeans Pdr." sold to Isaac McLeod, Teacher. So ended the formal education of the first pupil in whom the two schools co-operated.

Another entry in the academy records shows the registration of John and Flora Munro, children of John Munro, Esq. of St.

Ann's. A few years before, their talented uncle Alexander who for several years had been teaching at North Side St. Ann's had been forced to resign his school. The cause seems to have been a quarrel between the Munro brothers resulting from Alexander's failure to discipline his own children. His brothers, who were trustees of the school, engaged a teacher with inferior qualifications in his place, and Alexander set off with his brother-in-law, Norman McDonald, to investigate the possibilities of settling in Canada. Although they later returned to St. Ann's, Alexander Munro never again taught there. Probably the resultant decline of the school is reflected in the appearance of John Munro's children among the early registrants at the Boularderie Academy.

Although by 1839 the enrolment of Norman's school had decreased, its scope was constantly widening. There were forty-nine pupils, thirty-two in the common school and seventeen in the combined school, and, in addition to the subscription for the common school, the teacher received thirty-three pounds subscription for the combined school. In the combined school, Norman's sons, Alexander, now seventeen, and Murdoch, fifteen, had completed English grammar and were studying Euclid and algebra; Samuel, the thirteen-year-old, was studying Greek grammar, and the entry for Edward, a remarkable boy of nine, lists "Latin, Novum Testamentum and Greek grammar." The other students, varying in age from nine to thirteen, had just completed the common school and were all studying English grammar. In general the advanced school was entirely for boys, but here there may have been an exception. Although the record is not entirely clear, it appears that Peggy McLeod, who was now eleven, may once again have had a special privilege—this time of joining her brothers in the combined school and studying English grammar.

At this time the St. Ann's school was appearing in the correspondence of the Sydney office of the Commissioners of Schools. It was a problem of status and finance. The combined school, which had previously been classed as a first-class school, had during the last year been ranked only as second class. Mr. Ward, secretary of the Commission, interceded on behalf of the school. The law now was that the combined allowance should not be paid unless the teacher actually received, including the sum subscribed by the inhabitants and the allowance granted by the central government, a total sum of one hundred and twenty pounds in a school where fifteen or more scholars were taught. According to Mr. Ward's calculation, the total income of Norman's school, including the eighty-three pounds contributed by the inhabitants, and fifty-five from provincial allowances, was one hundred and twenty-eight pounds, which should have qualified the school for first class rating. Or, alternatively, the amount raised by the inhabitants, including the amount for the teacher's board and lodging, was ninety-two pounds, which, with the provincial allowance to the combined school, made a total of one hundred and twenty-seven pounds. However, since the sums allocated for board were not allowable, and since the provincial grant to common schools, was, instead of the usual twenty pounds, less than twelve, St. Ann's school did not meet the requirements and was rated as second class.

Whatever the provincial status of the school, the local fact stands out clearly that Norman's payment in the work of his neighbours had been doubled in the past ten years. It was not surprising that his two hundred acres of cleared land was becoming a model farm. To fathers of large families it must have seemed a very long time since they had become labourers on the McLeod farm. As with the years their awareness of their own dignity and security as landowners increased, their position must have seemed even more galling. Particularly when Norman's older sons, now young men in their middle twenties, were also superintending the operation of the farm. For Norman the men of the settlement still had the respect and fear that made their work an acceptable necessity. What duty did they owe these young men who had grown up among them, indulged by their father and ready to use to the utmost the protection of his name?

Although Norman's own school may have seemed one more tentacle wound around the life of his community, his genuine concern for education marked him out as a leader among the neighbouring settlements. They knew him as a man who could speak well and forcefully, who was not in the least intimidated by provincial authorities, and who was listened to with respect, if not always with approval. He was often requested to negotiate business for other communities. This he did simply and efficiently. To the Rev. Charles Inglis of Sydney, one of the Board of School Commissioners, he wrote on behalf of the neighbouring part of the Baddeck settlement.

St. Ann's, 18th March, 1840

Revd & dear Sir:

You will please to understand that the inhabitants of the upper Settlement of Baddeck having from time to time requested me to apply, in their behalf, to your Board of Commissioners for Schools, in order, if possible, to obtain provincial salary for another school besides the one already established in that quarter, I think it sufficient as an introduction on the subject to take the freedom of writing you only, and to inform you that the settlers of the said place find it quite impracticable for their children to attend at one school, especially during the winter, both on account of their increasing number, which, they tell me, is even now between 80 and 100, and the known inconvenience of their locality, particularly owing to a river that runs along the centre of the settlement from end to end and frequently overflows at a dangerous rate, without any proper bridge or other means of ferrying any wise answerable to the circumstance of one school. The distance of the place in question between the extremities about seven miles, of very indifferent Roads, which is indeed itself a formidable impediment, exclusive of the River. It is therefore humbly expected that you will find it a duty to consider the importance of the point in view and, if you think proper, to consult the rest of the Commissioners on the same ground, that at your convenience you may please to inform us of the consequence. If the wishes of the people concerned should succeed, the situation of the schoolhouses would, of course, be fixed by the Board of Commissioners, thro' the medium of some proper person in our neighbourhood, or at the mutual decision of the applicants themselves.

I am,
Rev'd & dear sir
Your Obt. Servt.
N. McLeod

Norman's influence in Cape Breton education was not only wide but enduring. His teaching in Gaelic was an important factor in the maintenance of a continuing Gaelic culture in the St. Ann's district for many years beyond the usual duration of Gaelic in Canadian communities. The language not only persisted, but continued in a much purer form than if it had been passed on orally and picked up only from home use. Teaching in Gaelic also produced a family solidarity that would have been impossible if the children of Gaelic-speaking parents learned only English at school. At St. Ann's the school child would sometimes be the first in the home to read laboriously from the Gaelic Bible to his illiterate parents or grandparents. They would be immensely proud of him, and by association, would attach to learning a sort of reverence, long reflected by Cape Breton Scots in their esteem of education.

Norman's influence persisted, too, in his students who went as teachers to the neighbouring communities. These teachers had no formal training but each of them had practice in hearing the lessons of the small children and supervising their behaviour. Such a monitor system was the only way in which nearly one hundred children in many different classes and stages could be taught in one schoolroom.

As in most of the early schools these bright senior students would be advanced at their own speed, progressing by their own efforts with the few minutes of tutorial help that their teacher could snatch from his hordes of juniors. Long after the others had been dismissed, these young men bent over their slates in the winter twilight and on the darkening trails muttered the theorem of Pythagoras or crushed the newly fallen snow to the stately measure of the *Aeneid.*

Norman's school had no frills for the average student. There was neither sewing nor singing there. But he had a leader's recognition of talent. In the young people he could enjoy it because it was his to control, to guide and develop. The young men to whom learning was in itself a challenge and a delight fared well in the competent hands of Norman McLeod.

CHAPTER NINE

The Master's Household

AS THE FAMILY of the community's head, Norman's children were necessarily in the limelight, but without the security of position enjoyed by the children of the old Scottish chieftains. When the chief's position was hereditary, his sons were automatically in training for future rule. The sons of a self-made chief had no such rights or expectations. Yet it was inevitable that in the shadow of their father's position they should act like heirs to his throne. It was equally inevitable that his people would not happily accept the transference to his family of the power which Norman had won only in his own right.

There would be many years, however, before the life of the McLeod family disturbed the community, years when the house at Black Cove enclosed all the doings of the ten children. The eldest was John Grant, the baby whose baptism had been so troublesome in Scotland. Then Donald, and Bunyan who had just been born when his father left Lochbroom for America. Perhaps it was the hard winter when Mary cared for the three little boys alone in Scotland, the long Atlantic crossing in the stifling fetid air of the ship, or the change from the climate of Scotland to Pictou which permanently injured his health. Bunyan was a gentle, delicate boy, happier with his mother in the house or poring over his books by the fire than playing outdoors with his lively brothers. He died in 1838 when he was twenty-one years old. His little sister, Mary, was a stronger child. She was born in Pictou the year after her mother and the boys came from Scotland, and, in her mother's arms, came safely through the shipwreck on Prince Edward Island and the rough journey through the strait toward St. Ann's.

Alexander, whom they called Sandy at home, was born

when they had been settled for a year in their cabin at the head of the harbour. Then came Murdoch, Samuel and Edward. It was little more than a year after Edward's birth that Margaret was born, a rosy happy child who immediately became Peggy to everyone, even her stern father. She was taking her first uncertain steps the next summer when her brother Edward died and they dug the small grave on the hillside and marked it with the curt epitaph, "Short spring; Endless autumn." It was little Peggy who could go to her grieving parents and tease the younger boys out of their bewilderment. She would never lose this special place in the family.

The next year, when she was forty-three years old, Mary McLeod had her tenth child. This boy, as was often the custom in that time, they named Edward in memory of the little son who had died. With the exception of Bunyan, the children were strong and healthy, but their mother's health was seriously impaired. She had never been a robust woman, and her life had demanded great physical strength. For her exhaustion there were emotional causes, too. She had lived with Norman for nearly twenty years. He loved and cared for her as a strong person for a weak one, but she could have no real share in his life. Although in his letters he often laments her poor health, his insistence upon it might imply that he preferred that his wife should be fragile and, once she had fulfilled her function in bearing his children, should be thus relegated to a minor position. For her, an intelligent woman who could not share in her husband's work nor direct the upbringing of her own children, what recourse was there but to be delicate?

After her first difficult years Mary McLeod did not have to endure the physical hardships of pioneer life. Domestic help was always available as a voluntary service from the community. When they had been about ten years at St. Ann's, Norman had sawn lumber brought from Pictou to build a large three-storey house. From that time they had a housekeeper as well as their other help.

It was a few years after Edward's birth that Norman wrote to his friend in Pictou: "I should be humbly thankful to the Lord for the degree of health that my dear Mary enjoys at this time altho she is never expected to be but delicate. The boy Bunyan is still but very tender, yet not always uncomfortable. He is generally improving his literal knowledge by study and reading altho much confined to the house since the beginning of winter.... My poor partner, tender as her frame is, would be glad to accompany me (to Pictou) if her health should in any way recruit. I would think it very agreeable to her constitution and to that of my sickly boy to take a short summer voyage, and this could not fail being a strong inducement to my mind on the subject. I have been away with them at sea for the space of a week in the beginning of August—and it was remarkably known that they both rapidly improved their health. I sorely regretted that my duties at home would not then admit of a longer stay upon the floating element."[1]

The words of a solicitous husband and father! Undoubtedly a week at sea was good for Mary, but surely it was also good for her that Norman was away from his duties at home. There could be no harder position for a sensitive woman than to be married to a man who felt a ruthless responsibility for his entire community. Inevitably there were smouldering antagonisms, which his purposeful strength could ignore, to prey upon her gentle spirit—outbursts of human feeling which neither her religious certainty nor her devotion to Norman could easily brush aside.

With unfailing regularity his letters report each time after his return from a trip that his "delicate spouse" during his absence enjoyed better health. On another occasion when he had been ill for several months he wrote that "my dear and delicate partner has had the mercy of enjoying better health during my illness than for several years past." Surely natural reactions of a woman who was not usually allowed her rightful measure of authority. More than once it seemed that Mary McLeod's mind was weakening. Norman mentions her "half dreaming notions of venturing along with me to Pictou to see several of her friendly acquaintances...but this fond view has far more of the will than of any appearance of its actual accomplishment." Later, as a sign of her great improvement he reports that "she has

[1] Harvey, D. C., ed., *Letters of Rev. Norman McLeod*, p. 5.

been enabled to attend both our public and private meetings for the last two or three Sabbaths, among a throng of people, which we thought a very singular & unlikely privilege...."[2]

Apparently, she had for some time found it impossible to endure attendance at church. But was it only the physical presence of the crowd? There was the day when Norman had named her publicly from the pulpit, for a very little sin—having a soberly ribboned bonnet sent from Sydney! For the first time she must have fully realized how the spirits of the people shrivelled as they sat and silently accepted the shafts they could not return. She had heard men of the congregation singled out and bitterly abused by Norman, but for such reproofs she would be able to find some cause. She had always been sorry to see the young girls publicly shamed for a few harmless ribbons. The bonnet seemed an innocent thing—she must have felt old and tired and wanted something pretty. Surely if the minister's wife wore a bonnet, the others, too, could discard without reproof the simple head scarves which at first they had all worn! In this, too, she failed. Her shame was not only in reproved vanity, but in being exposed deliberately and scornfully before a thousand staring people by her husband who had talked so solicitously of his "poor partner" and her delicate health. It helped not at all that she knew many of them to be suffering with her. She could not accept their pity. It was not surprising that the gentle Mary, overwhelmed by such harshness, should have at times lost "the peace of her mind."

Women were ill-fitting pieces in the pattern of Norman's life. Often, in writing of religious revivals, orgies of ill-directed enthusiasm which he scorned, he appraised the value of female conversions. He never failed to imply that they were easy converts because they fell in love with the preacher. In one of his letters to a young friend who wrote of the large number of converts in his home parish he jestingly wrote: "Could the Church but be advised to send forth a parcel of fleshy flippant flashy flirts as Missionaries, in the track of all your male Teachers, I should fondly anticipate and fully insure their proportionate success among our sex. There is an anagogical and a special

[2] ibid., p. 23.

analogy between the natural and religious influence of sexuality of which, I fear, many of our good clergy are not sufficiently aware; not so much from their lack of learning as from that of reflection. It is almost as rational for you to expect procreation in the animal world without sexual reciprocation as religious conversion among the male of our species—according to the ordinary spirit of our revivals—without sexual community or alternity in the ministry."[3]

Behind the facetious tone, is there an undercurrent of personal truth? He was completely aware of the potential attraction of the preacher. He not only scorned to use it, but counteracted it by lashing out in sadistic abuse of women, always focusing his attack on their ways of making themselves physically attractive. Intensity and passion which had marked his whole life were intellectually and spiritually acceptable, but in his stern doctrine the flesh was vile and Eve was the temptress.

The one attractive girl on whom Norman could without self-reproach lavish his affection was his charming daughter, Peggy. She had all his own fearlessness, and with it the vivacity and charm which endeared her to the whole community. Everyone expected excitement from Peggy McLeod, but it was about Mary, the older and quieter daughter, that there broke one of the most violent storms of the settlement.

Not far from the McLeods lived Squire Donald McLeod, Norman's long-time friend and associate in the building of the settlement. Donald McLeod took an important part in the religious affairs of the community, he was one of the three trustees of the school, and, after the rights of clergymen as magistrates were revoked, he succeeded Norman as a magistrate. On business and as a friend he came frequently to Norman's home and their children, who attended school and church together, had always been friends.

In their school days, Mary McLeod would seem a mere child to the Squire's son Luther who was four years older, but the time came when he realized that she had grown up. When he came casually to call at her home there was no chance for even a word with Mary alone. Her family still treated her as a

[3] McLeod, op. cit., p. 82.

PHOTOGRAPHS OF THE SHIPS' SURVIVORS AT THEIR 1903 REUNION

They called themselves "Eòin a' Chuan"—"The Sea Birds"

MARGARET

BACK ROW: R. Campbell (Waipu), J. J. McKay "Ian Ruadh" (Wpu.), P. H. McKay "Ian Ruadh" (Wpu.), A. J. McKay "Ian Ruadh" (Wpu.), J. M. McKay "Sean Rory" (Wpu.), Capt. G. McLeod (Whangarei Heads), Donald McGregor (Whg. Hds.).

MIDDLE ROW: H. Sutherland (Wpu.), D. McKay "Ian Ruadh" (Wpu.), Norman McKay "Ian Ruadh" (Wpu.), Donald McKay "Rory Og" (Wpu.), M. Fraser (Wpu.), James McInnis (Wpu.).

FRONT ROW: J. McLeod (Kau., Mrs. Paul (Whg. Hds.), Mrs. Lang (Wpu.), Mrs. A. J. Finlayson (Wpu.), Mrs. R. McKenzie (Wpu.), Mrs. H. Fraser (Wpu.), Mrs. Fenton (Wpu.), Mrs. M. W. McKenzie (Wpu.), J. Sutherland (Wpu.)

HIGHLAND LASS

BACK ROW: J. McKay "Ban" (Napier), D. McKay "Ban" (Wpu.), W. McDonald (Wpu.), Dan McKay "Ban" (Wpu.), K. McDonald (Wpu.), D. H. McKenzie (Wpu.), K. Stewart (Hds.).

THIRD ROW: Miss J. McKenzie (Wpu.), Miss C. McKay (Wpu.), Mrs. J. W. Durham (Wpu.), A. McKay "Ban" (Wpu.), N. McKenzie "Prince" (Wpu.), W. McLennan (Wpu.), J. R. McKay (Wpu.), Miss E. McKay "Ban" (Wpu.), Mrs. Webster (Wpu.), Mrs. R. Campbell (Wpu.).

SECOND ROW: H. McKenzie (Wpu.), R. Finlayson (Wpu.), Mrs. P. H. McKay (Wpu.), Mrs. Anderson (Mge.), Mrs. Sheddon (Auckland), Mrs. W. McKenzie (Wpu.), Mrs. D. McKenzie "Prince" (Wpu.), Mrs. J. Finlayson (Wpu.), Mrs. D. McLeod (Wpu.), Mrs. M. McAulay (Wpu.).

FRONT ROW: D. McKay "Ban" (Wpu.), Capt. J. McKenzie "Prince" (Wpu.), J. McLean (Wpu.), D. Stewart (Whg. Hds.).

Brig *Gertrude*, 215 tons, arrived Auckland, December 1856

Barque *Breadalbane*, 224 tons, arrived May 21, 1858

Brigantine *Spray*, 107 tons, arrived June 25, 1857

Barque *Ellen Lewis*, 336 tons, arrived May 11, 1860

PHOTOGRAPHS OF THE SHIPS' SURVIVORS AT THEIR 1903 REUNION

GERTRUDE

BACK ROW: J. Morrison (Wpu.), J. McLeod (Wpu.), Unknown.

THIRD ROW: Capt. J. Smith (Akd.), Mrs. Smith (Akd.), Mrs. Urquhart (Wpu.), N. Campbell (Wpu.), A. McMillan (Wpu.), A. McInnis (Wpu.), K. McDonald (Whg. Hds.), J. McMillan (Wpu.), A. P. Campbell (Wpu.), Miss Mary McKenzie (Wpu.).

SECOND ROW: J. Campbell (T.M.B.), Mrs. Brooks (Wpu.), Miss M. Morrison (Wpu.), N. J. Campbell (Wpu.), Mrs. M. McDonald (Wpu.), D. C. McLennan (Wpu.), Mrs. J. M. McKay (Wpu.), Miss M. McMillan (Wpu.).

FRONT ROW: Mrs. E. McLean (Wpu.), Mrs. N. McLean (Whg.), Mrs. J. Campbell (T.M.B.), M. Buchanan (Kau.), Mrs. N. McLennan (Kau.), Mrs. R. McKay (Kau.), Miss C. McLennan (Wpu.), Mrs. J. Wilson (Whg.), Miss B. Morrison (Wpu.), Mrs. E. McMillan (Wpu.), E. McMillan (Wpu.), Mrs. McKenzie "Shoemaker" (Wpu.).

SPRAY

BACK ROW: J. McKenzie (Kau.), Ewen McLean (Wpu.), K. Campbell "Buchan" (Wpu.), K. Stewart (Hakaru).

MIDDLE ROW: J. Cameron (Wpu.), A. G. McKenzie (Kau.), N. McKenzie (Kau.), M. W. McKenzie (Wpu.), Angus Stewart (Hak.), K. Stewart (Whg. Hds.).

FRONT ROW: Mrs. K. McKenzie (Akd.), A. Matheson (Omaha), Mrs. D. Finlayson (Wpu.), Mrs. W. Young (Om.), Mrs. D. McKay (Wpu.), Mrs. J. J. McKay (Wpu.), Mrs. D. McDonald (Whg.), Mrs. J. McLeod (Wpu.).

PHOTOGRAPHS OF THE SHIPS' SURVIVORS AT THEIR 1903 REUNION

BREADALBANE

BACK ROW: H. Sutherland (Wpu.), J. D. McKenzie (Whg.), N. McInnis (Kau.), J. R. McInnis (Kau.), N. McInnis (Kau.), D. McLean (Wpu.), N. McLean (Whg.).

FOURTH ROW: J. R. McLean (Wpu.), M. McDonald (Wpu.), M. McInnis (Kau.), Mrs. M. McInnis (Kau.), Mrs. Bishop (Wpu.), A. Fraser (Wpu.), D. McDonald (Wpu.), Mrs. W. McDonald (Wpu.), K. McAulay (Wpu.).

THIRD ROW: Mrs. A. Kempt (Wpu.), Mrs. H. Sutherland (Wpu.), Mrs. A. McKay (Wpu.), Mrs. Wykes (Akd.) Mrs. J. McMillan (Whg.), Mrs. Gill (Wpu.), Mrs. Fleet (Wpu.), Miss N. McLeod (Whg. Hds.).

SECOND ROW: Mrs. W. McKenzie (Wpu.), W. McKenzie (Wpu.), J. McKenzie (Okaihau), Mrs. J. McKenzie (Oku.), Mrs. J. McLean (Wpu.), J. McLean (Wpu.), Mrs. J. White (Oku.), Miss McLeod (Whg. Hds.), Mrs. A. Munro (Whg. Hds.), Mrs. A. McLeod (Wpu.), R. McLean (Wpu.).

FRONT ROW (holding picture): Mrs. J. McRae (Whg.).

ELLEN LEWIS

BACK ROW: A. McDonald (Whg.), A. McLeod (Kau.), D. A. McMillan (Wpu.), A. Kempt (Wpu.), J. McAulay (Wpu.), J. McLeod (Wpu.), A. McLeod (Wpu.).

THIRD ROW: D. M. McLeod (Wpu.), R. McRae (Wpu.), Mrs. McLeod (Wpu.), Mrs. N. Campbell (Mangawai), J. Kempt (Wpu.), N. H. Campbell (Wpu.), M. McLean (Akd.), J. McKenzie (Kau.), M. McDonald (Whg.), H. Ferguson (Tutukaka), J. Campbell (Wpu.), D. McLeod (Kau.).

SECOND ROW: Mrs. K. McKenzie (Wpu.), Mrs. Poulter (Akd.), Mrs. Wallace (Wpu.), Mrs. R. McGregor (Wpu.), Miss A. McKenzie (Wpu.), Mrs. K. Stewart (Whg. Hds.), Mrs. N. McKenzie (Kau.), Mrs. Kelsey (Wpu.), Mrs. H. Ferguson (T'kaka), D. Matheson (Kau.), Mrs. G. Ross (Whg. Hds.), Mrs. G. Sutherland (Wpu.), Mrs. F. Young (Wpu.).

FRONT ROW: First person unknown, Mrs. R. McRae (Wpu.), Mrs. J. Kempt (Wpu.), Mrs. H. McKenzie (Kau.), Mrs. J. McDonald (Whg.), Mrs. A. McMillan (Wpu.), J. McLean (Akd.), Mrs. McBeth (Kau.), Mrs. N. J. Campbell (Wpu.), Mrs. H. Sutherland (Wpu.), Mrs. N. McKenzie (Wpu.), Mrs. J. Munro (Marsden Point), Mrs. J. Munro (Wpu.).

child, and her father made it obvious that Luther's visits might be with the boys at the barns or on the wharf but they had no place in the house. Mary was a shy timid girl; she would not dare to risk her father's anger by slipping out to meet Luther. Finally, in desperation, Luther told the problem to his father and asked for his help in exchanging letters with Mary.

The Squire hesitated at first to deceive Mary's parents, but he knew how many things—often simple, joyful things—had to be concealed from Norman. He knew that there had been times when in his absence the attic of Norman's own house had rocked to his children's dancing feet and the mad music of the fiddle was heard even through the tightly closed windows. There had been times when the Squire himself had found it his duty to carry the tales that summoned transgressors for reproach, but he could not feel that there was anything essentially sinful in Luther's request that he take his letters to Mary. No doubt the old Squire weighed, too, the advantages of an alliance between his family and Norman's. It was already noticeable that, although the rule at Norman's home might be very strict, he never subjected his children to public reproof or indeed publicly admitted their faults. Presumably there would be a kind of immunity for any man who married into the family. Mary, shy as she was, would not get out from under her father's thumb without some help. The Squire on his next visit carried to Mary a letter from Luther. For some months the plan worked perfectly. Then Norman found out.

Norman in describing the incident to a correspondent in Scotland was harshly critical not only of this action but of the whole life of his old friend, the Squire. In him he found "a want of due command over his family, including his wife, his children and other domestics, so that his and their conduct has been a public discredit to his moral and religious character in every place of his residence during his religious life." He also complained of "an ungoverned tongue in him and them and a high degree of lordliness over their neighbours" and of "the keenest eye to detect and the sharpest tongue to correct the foibles of others when clashing with his own interests while at the same time blind and dumb to his own and his family's flagrant offences." Ironically, many of these things were already felt of Norman, but it would be ten years before anyone would have the courage to say them.

The incident seems a very personal matter between the two young people and their families. But Norman was chief of the community and the Squire was guilty of a plot against his chief. Norman was the divine representative, responsible to God for the community, and the Squire had sinned in deceit and hypocrisy. On both counts his conduct was a public issue. With self-righteous precision, Norman described the offence and its outcome: "On account of the proud, foolish and offensive conduct of his family, I could never have brought myself to allow any matrimonial connection taking place between his and my children; but he being of a different mind on this point and knowing both my own and my partner's inclinations to be the reverse of his, had secretly laboured to impose upon the mind of my daughter in favour of one of his sons; making her believe that he had Scriptures to that purpose from the Lord; and that by degrees her parents would acquiesce, till he was on the point of nearly tempting the poor girl to elopement with his son; and all this without my family's most distant knowledge till one of my good neighbours who was connected with his family told me of the plot; which was immediately overset. Let it now be observed that my religious friend had been during all the period of this clandestine wooing in the closest apparent friendship with me and my partner, embracing and kissing me from time to time with the sincerest seeming affection; and also praying and singing psalms and religiously conferring with me from week to week and from Sabbath to Sabbath, till on the discovery of his deceit and hypocrisy he was brought to a public trial, where his own letters on the subject, besides other means, were sufficient and irresistible evidence against him.

"On this shameful detection and when all his insinuating and evasive arguments could not serve him, he sobbed and sunk in a fainting fit in the throng meeting of our neighbours by whom the case was tried. And being brought home by the assistance of his family he kept his bed for several weeks together; acknowledging his fault and craving forgiveness; upon the apparent repentance of which, we, blessed be the Lord, felt no difficulty or reluctance in freely forgiving and forgetting all his offences. Yea, I humbly and meekly visited, and sincerely prayed with and for him in his confinement with a joyful and thankful heart in fond expectation of his moral and religious improvement as well as physical restoration. He recovered by degrees and was restored to all his former privileges, but he soon returned to his old ways and we at last refused him any private religious fellowship. After some tossings to and fro he went back to the Church of Scotland (which he had opposed for thirty years)."[4]

This letter Norman published a few years after the trouble.

Despite his long contribution to the building of the settlement, the old Squire was to be ousted. Norman had no authority over his position as magistrate, but he could attempt to uproot him as school trustee. The school rebellion of Luther's younger brother Isaac was added fuel for this fire. The school report of 1839 was signed by John McLeod instead of Donald McLeod with a note from Norman that "the other trustees and the subscribers for the school, in general, as well as myself" thought it necessary and desirable that this change should be made. The Sydney office, however, refused to allow it. They could hardly dismiss a trustee on the request of his presumed employee, the teacher! In reply to the Commission's refusal to replace the Squire, Norman pointed out that it would be difficult to ask or expect Donald McLeod to visit the school since "it is publicly known that I have thought it my grievous and indispensable duty with the deliberate consent and approbation of the better part of our community and the more judicious members of his family (possibly his son-in-law, John Fraser who was also a trustee), for very clear and urgent reasons to see him suspended from all our private religious association, and he has now of his own accord for some time declined to attend our public worship on the Sabbath and has not once visited our school since a twelvemonth."[5]

There had been many other times when offenders had been

[4] ibid., p. 89.

[5] Cape Breton School Papers.

disciplined but now a strong man had been broken in Norman's interpretation of the best interests of the settlement. For the first time he openly identified the maintenance of his personal power with the good of the community. The leader was turning dictator. Aware of the change, his people accepted it—some unquestioning in their devotion, others critical, but temporarily acquiescent in it as a necessary condition of the life they had chosen. The doubters could take refuge in the sly undercurrent of wit with which the Scot can maintain his inner ascendancy over his assumed superiors.

A few years before, Squire Donald had met on the road his friend and neighbour, Mrs. Norman McDonald, at the time when her husband was discontented and out of favour with the minister. "Is it yourself, Jane?" asked the Squire. "And who else?" retorted Jane. "I was thinking you'd be off to hide in a black hut in Africa. That's where I'd be going if I was on the outs with the Man." Now it was Jane's turn. "Well, Donald," she asked, "when are you for Africa?"

Presently Mary McLeod married Roderick Ross, a young man of her own age, a classmate through school, whose father was another of the small group of friends who had come with Norman to begin the settlement at St. Ann's. Roderick seems to have been completely acceptable to his father-in-law. He was a Justice of the Peace in Cape Breton, and after the migration, became a member of the New Zealand Parliament.

The gossip about the Squire had not yet died when a member of Norman's own family acted in a way that would certainly have been censurable in any other household in the community. Following John Munro's successful ventures in shipbuilding and trading, Norman's sons, John and Murdoch, began in 1838 the building of their first ship. This vessel, a 90-ton ship called the *Maria*, was completed the following year. Donald McLeod, the second son of the family, was placed in charge of her, and instructed to sell both cargo and ship in Glasgow. Donald did not return, and was to remain unheard of for many years.

This was not the last trading venture by the McLeod boys. They built other ships and carried various cargoes. In one of his open letters to Norman, published in the *Cape Breton Spectator* of March 1849, John Munro gives his version of their brandy-smuggling from the French island of St. Pierre. "If any other people were, as your sons were, last summer, landing, on mid-day Sabbath, their casks of 'French stuff,' when one of them went to Polly to get an empty bottle to give some of the 'creature' to the creatures that helped them, which Polly refused, in consideration of the day, but the intrepid 'smug' was not to be so thwarted but snatched a tea-pot from her dresser and decamped! But to go on with my supposition—if Squire McLeod's sons, or any other of the opposition, had been so employed on a week day, putting Sabbath aside, good Lord, deliver us, you would have required a bandage round your head for fear of its cracking! But we must plead 'necessity which has no law' as well as it is 'the mother of invention' in palliation for landing 'the French stuff' on the Lord's day as the vessel was bound, perhaps, for another port and could not wait until Monday, or, being trained under the tuition of an 'old Seneca' they would know the benefit of the maxim,—'Never leave till to-morrow that which you can do today.' It is not known what a day may bring forth—and on Monday, for aught they knew, a 'Tom Cat' might be mewing at their heels!"

Munro accuses Norman, too, of letting his family grow up as a bad example, "corrupting the youthful morals of those around them, without any restrictions, in direct opposition to your mode of discipline with regard to others.... It would have been better for you to have been grubbing out of them the symptoms of the debaucheries of the present day than panting to become a Cranmer or a Latimer."

John Munro believed that he had been wronged and was speaking from his bitter indignation, but tradition supports his estimate of the McLeod boys. They were bright lads, they had been given all the available advantages of education and allowed to stay regularly in school long after most young men in the settlement, but there is no record of their making any durable contribution to Cape Breton life. Time was not lacking, since John was thirty-eight years old when they sailed to Australia. It may also be significant that none of Norman's sons married in Cape Breton. It would seem that, even though they were indulged, they were also dominated so completely that a swaggering roguery was their only way of asserting their individuality. They may have been as their father was forty years before, but now they were barred by his strength from finding their own. Penalized by his power, it was only natural that they should also use it to the limit.

CHAPTER TEN

Hero-tyrant of St. Ann's

"NORMANISM," the outsiders called the religious practice of the people of St. Ann's, and Normanism it presently became, to them and to their leader. Among hundreds of McLeods, McLeod-ism would have been meaningless. For Norman it would also have been unsatisfactory. He liked to refer to himself by his Christian name and by doing so to see himself as a successor to Paul and the other apostles. Probably Paul was his ideal. He quoted him profusely and emulated him in his writing of admonitory epistles to his followers at Pictou and to his fellow clergymen, in his strong single-handed leadership and in his intense responsibility for all aspects of his people's lives.

To outsiders who heard Norman's abuse of their clergy and of the organized Church it seemed that Normanism was a negative thing which existed only in opposition. But the high ideal against which he battered other groups Norman also held for his own people, fighting down in their behaviour every sort of human impulse that could conflict with a high spiritual purpose, and so convinced of the greatness of his cause that there was no limit to the meticulous ruthlessness of his warfare.

Every detail of the observance of the Sabbath he supervised with careful concern. Nothing but the work of necessity could be done on Sunday. The potatoes were peeled on Saturday, and the dishes left unwashed until Monday morning. To drink from the brook or pick an apple from a tree was forbidden. The children learned to evade the second restriction by leaving apples on the lowest bough at the right height so that they could stand below and sink their teeth in them with their hands clasped innocently behind their backs. The dangling cores were proof that the fruit had not been "picked." The settlers were not even allowed to profit by nature's Sunday work. Each Saturday evening in the maple sugar season they had to make the rounds of their trees, and upset the sap troughs so that they would not use the Sunday run of sap. If, on a Sunday walk, a boy discovered where a hen had hidden her nest, he must leave the eggs untouched but carefully remember their location till Monday morning.

Even necessity was not an acceptable excuse if there was undue pleasure in the deed. One Sunday after the bay was frozen over, two boys skated to church. They were ordered to cut a hole in the ice and throw in their skates. The cutting of the holes was apparently acceptable Sabbath labour. During the summer it was permissible to come to church by boat, and at any time, to ride a horse at a decorous speed.

In the strictest households only theological topics were suitable for Sunday conversation. The adults discussed the minister's sermon and the children studied the catechism. Norman recalled as an example of clerical degeneracy a visit to a Scottish manse where "after dinner, on a Lord's day, the samplers of his Reverence's daughters were brought forward around the table for inspection."

Since the church service was one of the few public events of the week, another offence associated with the Sabbath was extravagance in dress. "The greatest zeal and zest for the Lord's day among the run of our youth," wrote Norman, "is evidently in order to see and be seen to advantage." He even went back to Noah's time to demonstrate that immodest dressing was a provocation for the Flood. "The sons of God saw the daughters of men that they were fair"—that is, in Norman's terms, "immodestly dressed to tempt and tease the carnal and careless powers and passions of their fickle and foolish spectators." So he condemned as instruments of Satan the girls' gay bonnets and flowing sleeves. There is no better evidence of the spirit of the community than that the women continued to attend church but also continued to wear their bonnets, although more than one girl started bravely from home in her new bonnet and hid it in a bush by the roadside rather than face the minister's scorn.

Often Norman had assailed the Church of Scotland for the laxity of its discipline. Its punishments were usually confined to breaches of the seventh commandment, "Thou shalt not commit adultery," and the censure was often commuted for money. If the offenders were censured it was in the comparative privacy of the Session room, not before all.

Norman showed no such mercy, but so great was the fear of him that there was never an occasion for the public censure of adultery. The only family which was known to have a guilty member moved from the settlement before they had to face the public humiliation. For other offences there was opportunity for merciless public reproof. Before the whole community Norman forced the abasement of Donald McLeod. For vanity and conspicuous dress he indicted even his own wife.

It had long been the custom of Presbyterian preachers to single out evildoers in the congregation. With mystical intensity the ominous words would hover over the people, "There is one here who convicts himself of sin...." In vaguely suggestive theological terms, comprehensible only to the person addressed, the sin would be described and the guilty man would inwardly cringe. Such obscurity was not for Norman. He named individuals and from the pulpit poured his scorn and vituperation upon them.

In one of his public letters of 1849 John Munro relates Norman's vicious persecution of John Fraser whom he publicly accused of being everything that was deformed in mind and body. As Munro tells it, it is an ugly story. He infers that Norman attacked Fraser who was a Justice of the Peace, not for any real sins or faults of character, but only in the interests of his mighty son-in-law, Roderick Ross, who was also a J.P. He claims, too, that the only way for John Fraser to rid himself of this public abuse was to turn informer against the old Squire McLeod, his father-in-law. For this weakness Munro would not wholly condemn him, for, he says, "You would find many a man who would gallantly encounter the field of battle that would shudder at the idea of being caricatured into a ridiculous monster in the presence of hundreds of strange faces, in a church."[1]

Every Sunday there would be hundreds of spectators. From all sides of St. Ann's they came, from North River and North

[1] *Cape Breton Spectator,* 1849.

Shore, along the coast from Cape Smoky, or from Whycocomagh far up the lake they started on Friday for their long journey to church. They came by boat across the harbour, on foot in solemn dark lines along the forest trails, in wagons and sleighs in the later days of roads. The small frame building which in 1822 had seemed more than adequate for the first settlement was soon overflowing. In the summer, services were held on the hillside by the church, but the winter congregation must have been sorely crowded before the large new church was completed, more than twenty years later. The new building contained seats for twelve hundred people, but within two years, it, too, was too small, even its stairs and passages overcrowded.

Tall and plain, it stood at the little inlet of Black Cove, near the minister's house at the head of the harbour, close to the site of the first church. Sixty feet long and forty feet wide with twenty-foot walls, it towered over the old church and even over Norman's large house. There were four entrances to the ground floor and two stairways to the galleries which ran around three sides of the building. The church was finished throughout, and the floor sloped gradually toward the front of the auditorium. Each of the windows, about six feet high, was skilfully arched, with its frame evenly grooved. Every detail showed the careful work of experienced carpenters who had been building boats and trading ships and would soon build the passenger vessels for the long voyage to Australia.

The manual labour of building the church was only one small part of the religious dues owed by the people of St. Ann's. As their minister, Norman refused any regular or fixed salary. Instead he received, as he did for his teaching, labour on his farm in the chopping, stumping and burning required to clear the land, and in the planting and harvesting which followed. The people also did the work of building Norman's barns and ships. Every adult man was required in these ways to support the "means of grace" in the community. Over all the work Norman had the final oversight.

It was necessarily upon the whole community that the duties were levied. Church membership could not be the basis of their responsibility, since Norman's church had no members in the usual understanding of the term. He never dispensed the Lord's Supper at St. Ann's. This omission was no indication of disrespect for the sacrament or of a low estimate of its value. Rather he believed it an ideal beyond the grasp of his people. He considered that in Scotland the sacraments had been constantly profaned by being casually dispensed to all who applied for them. He went to the other extreme. Instead of a profession of faith, he required clear evidence of spiritual regeneration and a high degree of holiness. Again and again he condemned the mere shell of formal profession, and pointed out how far beyond the attainment of frail human nature were real spiritual knowledge and discernment, true faith and repentance.

He particularly deplored the weakness of the Church of Scotland of his day in turning the "fencing" of the Communion table into a casual matter of form. In the old tradition of the Church, the fencing of the table meant a formidable dissertation upon Paul's terrible words: "Whosoever shall eat this bread and drink this cup of the Lord unworthily, shall be guilty of the body and blood of the Lord. But let a man examine himself, and so let him eat of that bread and drink of that cup. For he that eateth and drinketh unworthily eateth and drinketh damnation to himself." When it was offered on these terms, only those with unshakable confidence in the grace of God could dare partake of the Lord's Supper. It was, however, a tenet of the Calvinistic doctrine that each man, under God, was his own judge. By refusing communion to his people because he deemed them unworthy, or by giving them so mean an estimate of their own worth that they dared not ask for it, Norman assumed a spiritual dictatorship unjustified by the faith which he professed.

He made baptism equally unattainable. In Scotland under the Moderate regime in the church it was often the practice to accept any children for baptism, regardless of their parents' church membership or standards of conduct. For Norman, the parents' right of access to the Lord's table and their infants' right to baptism rested on the same authority. His refusal to baptize their children antagonized many parents who not only objected to the denial of the sacrament but felt that in its denial some measure of physical protection was being withheld from their child. Some of his people had their children baptized elsewhere but continued to attend his church.

Although his people were remarkably docile in the face of his methods, they did not all remain in meek subjection. About fifteen years after the settling of St. Ann's, Norman told his Pictou correspondent that Norman McDonald was considering leaving the settlement and had gone to Canada with a view to settling there. "He has been for many years dissatisfied, on religious accounts, & for a long time promised himself to gain a strong party to strengthen his foolish pretensions; but by degrees failing of success and more desperately of late, he thought proper at last to abandon this corner."[2]

McDonald was one of Norman's old friends from Assynt, a leader in the migration to St. Ann's, and his family had been educated with Norman's children from the beginning of the settlement. He and his wife were intelligent, aggressive people who would not accept the increasing tyranny of Norman's methods. Although McDonald did not leave permanently, two of his sons presently went to Canada and none of his children joined in the migration to Australia. Characteristically, Norman McLeod, even when he was losing a friend and an old associate, made no attempt to modify his actions or to achieve a compromise. Instead he wrote: "We were since a long time desirous to be rid of such malcontents whenever it would fall out in the course of providence."[3] As time passed, others, too, left the congregation because they could not endure his arbitrary methods. The majority, afraid of the world, secure in a traditional loyalty to the chief, remained in outward agreement with him and kept themselves within the safe framework of the community.

Only in the old tradition of the chief was there a parallel for some of his followers' devotion. One typical story is attributed to several followers, usually to John Smith of Indian Brook. Before Norman left on the great migration to Australia, he paid a farewell visit to Mr. Smith. After Norman had gone, Smith took down the door by which his venerated minister had en-

[2] Harvey, D. C., ed., *Letters of Rev. Norman McLeod*, p. 5.

[3] ibid., p. 5.

tered the house. He made another opening and fitted the door into it, for "no man might ever cross the threshold after Norman McLeod." Perhaps, when the story reached him, Norman thought of the old lady whom he had seen as a child in Assynt who would never again shake hands with any other after her right hand had been touched by a descendant of her chief. And still, more than a century after he left the island, there are people in Cape Breton who can remember in their childhood pious old men who never attended church. They had heard their last sermon when Norman sailed away, and forever after remained Norman's men.

It is difficult to identify the man who received such adoration with the tyrant who quenched the strong spirits of his congregation. Part of his success may have been that in him the weak and unlettered men saw, as well as their spiritual leader, their defence against the strong men of the community. Deep within the Scot, as deep as his own sustaining pride, lies his desire to see the mighty brought low. He slyly scoffs at the man who is "big feeling" and tries to convince himself that such men are of small account. Coinciding with this desire was Norman, with his Calvinistic certainty that man existed only for the glory of God, that all were equal in absolute depravity, and that man's confidence could lie only in his knowledge of his own spiritual election. As he assailed the strong and successful, he was the spokesman of the lesser men. His victims—Alexander Munro, Norman McDonald, Squire McLeod, John Fraser, John Munro, a roll-call of the strong men of the community—one by one were lashed by Norman's scorn. The men who had neither the ability nor the courage to excel or to revolt, might be allowed to continue mediocre and unnoticed, and, in their obscurity, secure.

The abuses inherent in his authoritarian control of the settlement many of the people accepted as natural necessities. They knew the tradition of supreme control by chiefs and later by landlords and clergy. The Church of Scotland, against which, with Norman, they were in revolt, was their only tradition of democratic government. By breaking away, they had separated themselves from its forms. In civil government they were not yet ready to take advantage of their new position as landholders. Many of them were scarcely aware of their new rights and certainly they were not ready to oppose them to a man who repeatedly declared that he feared no one but God, and who, by his actions, left no doubt that he spoke the truth.

They knew their need for leadership and authority. They could accept it with less sacrifice of pride from a man whose position was divinely sanctioned than from men whose ability and skill had raised them economically above their fellows. Of the minister's position Norman had informed them, "The clergy should be thought a singular set of men as by their office different from all other mankind, and therefore ought not to be deemed on a level with the rest of the species."[4] Norman, then, could honestly, in the name of his office, accept the homage of his people. And no homage could be too great for God's representative.

Such unquestioning obedience would be the price of Norman's favour. No compassion restrained him from public reproof of the strong who seemed in any way to oppose their will to his, but in a general letter to his loyal followers at Pictou he declined to reprove any specific personal failings. To his friend John Gordon, the leader of his people there, he wrote: "I find some inconvenience in writing to so many of you under the shape of one correspondent, because this circumstance will not admit of so much freedom in expressing my thoughts to you individually. For it is not so tolerable for you to hear of your particular or individual defects or dangers in letters open to all, as if you were respectively addressed alone or apart.... And we labour under another disadvantage in our correspondence, if I should ever turn my thoughts to address every one of you apart, the most of you cannot read, and hardly two among you would be able to express your minds freely and properly without recourse to other hands to return me answer. You may consequently feel assured that I use a considerable degree of reserve in my communication with you, and that I plainly see different traits in some of your characters & habits that are both very deep & dark, as well as very dangerous, of which I have never

[4] McLeod, op. cit., p. 73.

written you one word. And tho' you are in general my kind friends for a long time now, yet some of you are so self-conceited of your own wisdom & understanding, and so head-strong in your temper and disposition, that I should fear very much how far you could bear even a Christian plain dealing."[5] In his series of letters to Gordon there is only one in which he administers a personal reproof. That is for the presumption of "the vainglorious James" (Gordon) who had eulogized a member of his family with an ostentatious epitaph and a lavish gravestone, out of keeping with his "low and obscure circumstance."

It was not always easy for even the humblest of his followers to see in Norman's actions the will of God. A story of his judgment in a case of theft has become legendary in Cape Breton. One day a man of the settlement on his way to work met a pedlar from whom he bought some articles. Since he had no money with him, he returned home, taking the pedlar with him, and took from an unlocked chest a purse containing a considerable sum of money. He paid for the purchases, returned the purse to the chest and, with the pedlar, left the house. Soon afterward they separated. In the evening the purse was gone. The blame fell on a neighbour boy and he was urged to confess. Again and again he repeated that he knew nothing about it, but his inquisitors persisted. Finally they ordered that he should be locked in the graveyard for the night. He hesitated for a moment, but the terror was too great; he confessed to the theft. Immediately Norman passed sentence—a part of his ear was to be cut off. The sentence was carried out at once by one of his loyal followers.

The settlement was shocked by the crime but it did not utterly condemn the punishment. It was not many years since a man in Sydney had only at the last moment been reprieved from death for the crime of stealing an old coat which was stuffing a broken window. Thieves were still publicly whipped on the streets of Sydney, and the stocks and pillory were in use. Mutilation was a drastic punishment but it might be justified to keep the settlement pure.

[5] Harvey, D. C., ed., *Letters of Rev. Norman McLeod*, p. 9.

The climax came a week later. A witness admitted having seen the pedlar climbing out of the window of the house on the afternoon of the day when he had learned where the purse was kept. When he was caught he confessed that he had stolen it. The whole settlement turned from Norman in shame and horror at the boy's punishment.

Perhaps for the first time in his life Norman was afraid. He could not escape or transfer the responsibility for his summary judgment. He could hardly call his disastrous mistake the will of God. His act could mean the end of his authority in the community. Muffled in his heavy cloak, he went in the night to the father of the boy. What passed between them was never told. When the people gathered, curiously, in church the next Sunday, they heard a strange sermon. It was a mystical exaltation of a man who was presently recognizable as the father of the mutilated boy. No other reference to the crime and judgment was made by either Norman or the father, but presently it was told that a Sydney lawyer had volunteered to take action against Norman on the boy's behalf, and the father had refused because that would be going against God.

CHAPTER ELEVEN

Whips and Scorpions

"FAITHFUL are the wounds of a friend, but the kisses of an enemy are deceitful." This proverb set the rule for Norman's relationship with his associates just as surely as his position as their minister marked out his responsibility to his followers. Coupled with the proverb's justification for plain speaking was his constant and intent awareness of his position as one of God's elect. Once he had felt God's hand upon him marking him out, he could not shirk his responsibility toward any of his fellows nor could he allow any consideration for their feelings or fear of losing their friendship to deter him from his duty toward them. An aim essentially selfless and sincere, but carrying with it a dangerous temptation. Words intoxicated him; he loved to play with them and was vain of his skill, editing his wife's simple words and the sayings of his people into his own sonorous phrases, and criticizing the errors and redundancies in the publications of the Church. So as he set out to write to his fellow preachers, his pen turned to a sword and was wielded with fierce enjoyment.

To his former college friend, Rev. A. McLeod, still in Scotland, he wrote berating him for his enmity to Dissenters from the Established Church: "You never were by nature but a mere simpleton, or two-thirds of an idiot, and your false conversion, scraps of philosophy, fragments of divinity, painted parlour, dainty table, sable surtout, curled cravat, ponderous purse, big belly, poised pulpit, soft and silly spouse, the acclamation of fanatics and formalists, the association of kindred plagiarists and impostors, your seared conscience and a silent God have all conspired, no wonder poor man, to turn your mind to total forgetfulness and your head to eternal dizziness...."[1]

[1] McLeod, op. cit., p. 133.

Before the letter has ended he attempts to explain his words: "You have joined that very clergy whom you derided, despised and opposed; and never given me—your once faithful and fond companion—nor the public any reason for your solemn and sounding change. As to my bombastic and sarcastic style, I take the subject of my animadversion to be in some of its bearings a step far beyond serious treatment; and it would therefore be ridiculous and quite below the intention of these remarks to handle most of the desperate and heaven-abandoned characters in discussion but in a degree under the lash and line of satirical ordeal."[2]

Even strangers he scathingly upbraided. He published his correspondence with a minister from Inverness to whom he had written on behalf of a neighbouring Cape Breton community which wished to secure him as their pastor. The Scottish minister explained that he could not live on less than his present salary of two hundred pounds a year, and mentioned in apparent humility that he never felt equal to his office as minister. Norman lashed out at him:

"If you really think yourself not qualified you ought to resign your office.... You are not qualified, Sir, for your office, but you do not properly believe it, nor would you wish me or any other to believe it. Do you not know that one may be very humble-minded and yet very confident in the Lord and of his gracious and sovereign mercy?... You seem to my neighbours to be also pretty keen for the world, although you endeavour very slyly to disguise your principle on this head. You have played long enough among the simple to inure you to hypocrisy because your conscience is alarmingly dormant.... Do not think that I write at random—no, no, I know so much of my own deceit and duplicity by nature, that I find no difficulty in seeing through your letter, the very principle of your soul, for all your silly art to conceal it."[3]

Convinced of their innate depravity, Norman was a ruthless analyst, seeing through to the principles of men's souls. Once he had discovered the motives of his fellow preachers he readi-

[2] ibid., p. 135.
[3] ibid., p. 222.

ly chose to let his God-given duty to reveal his findings take precedence over the human charity of silence.

No words were too slighting for the other ministers of Cape Breton, "the very tag and tail of preaching." They all incurred his scorn, but his principal foe was the Rev. Peter McLean whose dramatic revival services at Whycocomagh stand as pinnacles in Cape Breton's religious history. Revivals Norman bitterly attacked. "They talk," he says, "of sin and duty in very vague and general terms; and of the Saviour at great random; their gloomy sorrow and smirky joy are both alike quite disagreeable to the lively and gentle spirit of the Gospel."[4] Their dramatic conversions he attributed to fear and emotional excitement, and scornfully told of a natural fool at Loch Inver in Assynt who was the subject of a revival there and later went about the village followed by curious children for whom he would repeat his "conversion-fits" for a halfpenny.

Again and again he ridiculed the visions and wild notions of the excited new converts. When one of them cried exultantly, "I'm a child of the King. The cattle on the thousand hills are mine," Norman flatly remarked, "You just try to milk one of them and see what happens." Anything connected with the irrational or supernatural he quickly brought down to earth. One day a lay preacher told him that in the past fifteen years there had been no event but he could foretell. Norman asked him how many pigs with their respective genders would comprise the brood of a sow before them about to litter. The lay preacher was so angry that he was ready to hit him.

He was equally annoying, for more profound reasons, to the ordained Presbyterian clergy of Cape Breton. Most of these ministers, almost all sponsored by Mrs. Mackay's Edinburgh Ladies' Association, had arrived on the island in the early 1830s. Norman's nearest neighbours were the Rev. James Fraser, an intelligent kindly man who had spent some years in business and European travel before studying theology and coming to Boularderie, and the Rev. Alexander Farquharson, who, after years in the army, had become a minister and was to spend the last twenty-five years of his life in the settlement of Middle

[4] ibid., p. 15.

River. To these men, as to Mr. McLean and their fellow clergymen, Norman was a constant annoyance. They found that people from their communities went on Sunday to Norman's church and heard him deriding the Church of Scotland which they represented. To them as individuals he applied his charges against all her clergy: "profanity of conversation and conduct, abuse of the Sacraments, and desecration of ecclesiastical ordination."

Since they were ostensibly of the same faith as Norman, and considered that he was undermining their work, it was their duty to challenge him. Yet they knew that none of them could match him in single combat if he chose to release all the resources of his caustic tongue. In 1836 they had organized as the Presbytery of Cape Breton, a presbytery of the Church of Scotland in Nova Scotia. Even this group hesitated for some time to remonstrate with Norman, but fiery, emotional Peter McLean in his revival services throughout the island was clashing with him more and more frequently and kept pressing for action. Finally in 1840 when they met to induct a minister at Broadcove they also composed the letter which was intended to bring Norman under their control.

To: Rev. Norman McLeod
St. Ann's
Cape Breton

Broadcove, September 24th, 1840

Reverend Sir:—

We, the undersigned, form the only Presbyterial and the highest ecclesiastical authority acknowledged by the Established Church of Scotland in this Island, and in that capacity possess jurisdiction over all the members, probationers and ministers of that church residing within the bounds of Cape Breton.

We have learned that you claim the status of a minister of that church. Therefore, we, in the exercise of the jurisdiction competent to us, call upon you to produce at the bar or before our Moderator, within forty days of this date, the documents on which you found your claim.

We add that in the event of no satisfactory credentials being within that time produced, we may at the expiration thereof feel ourselves called upon to take more public measures in reference to the claim you advance.[5]

We are, Rev. Sir,
Yours, etc.,
James Fraser, Moderator
Dugald McKichan, Clerk
John Gunn
Peter McLean
Alex. Farquharson

The letter reached Norman two weeks later. He went straight to his desk and slashed out his answer.

To: Rev. James Fraser
Boularderie Island
Cape Breton

St. Ann's, C.B., October 6th, 1840

Rev. Sir:—

Your letter of the 24th ult., signed at Broadcove by yourself and the rest of your Rev. brethren on the Island, I received this morning, to which I beg to answer that it requires a piece of self-denial in me to take any notice of such a fulminating farce; but the sacred proverb says, "Answer a fool according to his folly lest he be wise in his own conceit." And of all fools, I consider religious fools, at the pinnacle of the profession, to be the most dangerous to deal with, whose minds and consciences are so sadly and shamefully seared up to every mode of conviction of their own religious miscarriage.

I flatly deny having ever claimed the "status of a minister of the Church of Scotland," and in all humility and sincerity, desire to bless heaven for having enlightened my mind to dread and abhor that state.

I have certainly from time to time professed myself as, in my own estimation, a poor and unworthy member of the once venerable and glorious Church of Scotland; but the meagre, pitiful and

[5] ibid., p. 5.

degenerate thing that passes now under the pompous and bloated sanction of that name, I utterly and indignantly disclaim with all its alarming "bars" and awful "authority," in the most open and unreserved manner possible, so that you or any other cannot make this avowal more public than I freely allow, and without downright and wilful misrepresentation. I openly defy all the information in the country to substantiate anything beyond the scope of this plain declaration against me on the subject.

I feel no diffidence on this stable ground, and since ever I arrived at my conviction on these points, I have never felt desirous of evading candid and dispassionate investigation of them.

I do not wish to excite your anger, which is, alas! but too manifestly shown on the least occasion, but in consideration of your dangerous and wilful extravagance especially regarding the wild and fanatical changes, under the name of conversion, worked up by the silly and disgustful art of some of you and fostered by almost all of you, together with your openly profane and indiscriminate administration of the most solemn and sacred ordinances, exclusive of many similar means of conviction, in the obvious tenor and tendency of your conversation and conduct, I cannot but infer, without contradicting all scriptural reasoning on the point, that the Church that gives place and support to the like of your characters in her highest office must, in fact, be anything other than a living Church of Jesus Christ. This has been my most serious and deliberate view of the subject for the long space of forty years together, and every day confirms me more in this grievous though unavoidable determination.

O! the vast privilege and rare benefit of "forty days'" suspense and respite!

In fine, I heartily regret that your unfortunate, offensive and confirmed insolence and pride, so conspicuous in your letter as a true specimen of your general disposition and conduct as ministers towards all who dare object to your measures, render it morally impossible for me to answer you in a more agreeable style. "With the froward thou shalt shew thyself froward."[6]

I am, Rev. Sir, Yours, etc.,

Norman McLeod

[6] ibid., p. 6.

The Presbytery never wrote again, but Norman had more to say. From these two letters grew a book which he published in 1843 and entitled *The Present Church of Scotland and a Tint of Normanism Contending in a Dialogue.*

On its title-page he states, "It is designed that any Profit arising from the sale of this Pamphlet, after all necessary deductions, shall be duly contributed to the service of the British and Foreign Bible Society." The "pamphlet" is a 350-page book, grown to such a size, Norman explained to his friends, "under the procrastination of the Press." It began with a dialogue between men of different viewpoints in the Church of Scotland, and while the printers were delayed he added an assortment of material—quotations from theological works, copies of his own letters, and finally, comments on the disruption in the Church of Scotland which was taking place in the year of its publication. The result is that it "treats of various subjects besides the degeneracy of the Church of Scotland, altho' that was the original aim of it."

The tone of the book is set by the Scriptural quotations which appear on the title-page: "Not by might, nor by power, but by my spirit, saith the Lord of Hosts" (Zechariah iv. 6), and "The weapons of our warfare are not carnal but mighty through God" (2 Corinthians x. 4). The warfare between Norman and the Church of Scotland, in direct combat, and by allegory, insinuation and inference, is the connecting thread of the curious book.

Norman paid about 120 pounds to have a thousand copies printed in Halifax, and proposed to sell them for five shillings each. Buoyantly he wrote to John Gordon that he expected to send some hundreds of copies to Scotland and would like to have a list of the probable subscribers in Pictou in order that none of them would be disappointed.

It was Norman who was disappointed. He had been sure that "mere curiosity to see the production of the singular leader of the Normanists" would sell many copies of the book. But outsiders had learned to ignore him, and three years later he was writing to Pictou, "In order to release a degree of the money which my friends kindly borrowed for me there, I will allow you to sell the unsold books at a reduced price; or even at any price that you may think proper to set upon them." Still later, on the eve of his migration, he was collecting from Pictou the unsold copies of his book.

His friends told him that the book was too severe. This he refused to admit, claiming that "a generation hardened and aggravated against means of knowledge" required such severity, although they cared only for what would "soothe and flatter their own religious formalism and false confidence." It was typical of his lack of understanding of people that he should expect them to buy a book because, in his opinion, it would be good for them. Within his own community he could ruthlessly use his power to achieve his interpretation of the divine purpose. Where no one feared him, his words lay unheeded. Yet he would not change. A Calvinist zealot, he cared only for God's point of view; he could not strike a level that would appeal to men. Indeed, he might perversely have been dismayed if his defence of Normanism had been so successful that he could no longer savour the superiority of a martyr. To attack, to explain, and to exhort were consistent with his profession of Calvinism; to attempt to win men savoured of the Arminianism which he abhorred.

Although a reader would be likely to judge that it was only his pride in his own words which led him to publish his ill-arranged ill-assorted book, he claims a deeper pride as its source. He sincerely believed that he was God's instrument in correcting the sad condition into which the Church had fallen. "I, in my weak but sincere manner," he wrote, "thus endeavour to plead with my mother (the Church of Scotland), in the behalf and name of my Heavenly Father; since I see none of her children taking the doleful cause in hand. The Lord knows it is with a trembling and sorrowful heart I plead, with all my failings about my neck, of which I am, partly, sadly sensible; and with all the apparent sharpness, if not acrimony, of the spirit by which my poor pleadings are conducted; yet to which I humbly trust, my Heavenly Father in his providence, hath called me, after a long struggle and suspense, between fear and disgust—fear of myself—disgust of my mother's evil doings."[7]

[7] ibid., p. 59.

His protest against the Church of Scotland, not only in his book but in all his actions, was not only the protest of a reformer against the Church's evil doings. It was also the rebellion of a strong individual against the restraints which the corporate beliefs of an organization necessarily imposed upon his mind.

To him, dissent in religion always meant progress—from formalism and empty ritual toward plain truth. Even Jesus, he pointed out, was a dissenter in His day from the Church of His fathers and was for that reason condemned and crucified. All the Churches, too, were, in their origin, dissenting Churches—"the Church of England from popery, the Presbyterian from popery and prelacy, and the Independents from one another." He believed that from any man's study of the Bible there could come just basis for dissent. "When any man judiciously finds or forms a party...more agreeable in their sentiments and conduct to the plain rules of the sacred Scriptures than the community from which he separates, it is so far a favourable sign." "I most heartily abominate," he wrote, "the vain and wicked pretence to the private or peculiar privilege or right of any person or party on earth to the interpretation of the Word of God."[8] Infallibility he condemned as a wicked and deadly thing which of itself rendered it "a most necessary and imperative duty to any man to dissent from it."

Adherence to forms and codes in religion he styled "mental popery," one of the most dangerous errors among church people. "Most men care nothing for one Church or another but from mere habit and external circumstances," he wrote, "most people are of the religion of their parents; most communities are of the same denomination, loyal to the name rather than the doctrine of their party."[9]

Simplification of traditional forms did not in itself satisfy him. The Methodists he praised for their moral goodness and their persistent kindness, but he found in their emotional excess a lack of critical intelligence. "A few groans now and then," he explained, "a little frothy talk of your experience—a sly smile and looking aloft—to whistle a hymn—to be punctual at your

[8] ibid., p. 234.
[9] ibid., p. 237.

exercise of frivolous and fanciful devotion—and to turn your common conversation to Scripture phraseology—will make you a sound saint among the Wesleyans."[10]

There were no emotional excesses in his Baptist associates, whom as individuals he highly respected. Again he disapproved on intellectual grounds, not, this time, of the entire sect, but of the uneducated clergy who knew only the Bible and the concordance. He was disgusted, too, by their method of performing baptism—"The minister will lead his female subject to immersion in her bare smock or shift in the very face of a cluster of males and mocking spectators without the sign of a blush on the brow of either him or her."[11]

Anglican clergy he did not consider spiritual. "In England," he wrote, "the established clergy are, for the most part, trained up to their holy vocation in the same manner as to any secular calling and generally live as laymen do—hunting, shooting, card-playing, frequenting theatres, dancing at, and conducting, as masters of ceremonies, balls and assemblies, eating, drinking, cursing, swearing, electioneering...according to their means, ability and inclination, being distinguished from other mere worldlings by their exterior apparel, and not always even by that."[12]

There were few occasions for co-operation among members of various religious denominations in the scattered settlements of Cape Breton. When the need arose, Norman, despite his objections to their beliefs, worked more amicably with them than with his fellow Presbyterians. For the errors of other sects he felt no driving responsibility. It was only his own people who had cause to dread his ruthless sense of duty.

One organization in which all denominations shared was the Bible Society. It had been active in Nova Scotia at the time of Norman's arrival. In 1814 the Pictou society, promoted by Dr. McGregor, had sent seventy-five pounds to the parent society—fifty as a free contribution and twenty-five from the sale of Bibles. A generous sum from a pioneer community! As the

[10] ibid., p. 253.
[11] ibid., p. 292.
[12] ibid., p. 289.

general level of literacy rose, the demand for Bibles increased and the Bible Society's work was highly valued.

The Pictou group was presently reorganized as an auxiliary of the British & Foreign Bible Society with James Dawson, the first bookseller in the province outside Halifax, as their secretary and depositary. The people of St. Ann's with the Bible as the textbook of their schools were necessarily as good customers of the Society as their income would permit. Through their friends in Pictou they kept in contact with the organization there until in 1840 Norman established an auxiliary of the Society at St. Ann's.

Even in this work Norman conflicted with the other Presbyterian ministers on the island. He found the five ministers, he says, "a sore rebuff and a saddening check upon the activity and progress of the two best and grandest institutions under the stars—the Bible and Temperance Societies—not only by their shameful neutrality on these choice and exhilarating subjects, but what is worse, by openly vilifying and misrepresenting the motives and measures of the more zealous leaders in the country on this very ground, tolling and tempting the minds of not a few of our inhabitants, both by example and persuasion to stand aloof or fall away from these most eminent means of moral and religious...improvement."[13]

Even if some of the clergy were lukewarm, the Bible Society had general public support, but the temperance movement had a harder course. Norman had long been opposed to hard liquor. Whisky was familiar in Scotland, but in Pictou he had seen what excesses could be reached in the new world. Restraints were fewer, the proportion of carefree adventurers was higher, the cold climate was always an excuse, and cheap rum was pouring in from the West Indies as fast as they could drink it. In the war years, money had been more plentiful than ever before and the habit of heavy drinking was well established.

Its social and moral effects disturbed some community leaders, but when peacetime reduced the flow of money its drain on the people's income was a concern to all. The rum trade had been one of the reasons why Norman was eager to

[13] ibid., p. 107.

move his people away from Pictou. There were others who did not leave. Rev. Duncan Ross of Pictou, Norman's direct antithesis as a co-operative community leader, attempted to do something about it, and in 1827 he took the lead in organizing the first temperance society in Nova Scotia.

If anyone could have made an unpopular movement popular it would have been Mr. Ross. He was a man of cheerful common sense, a leader who was never afraid to make an intelligent compromise. Shortly before Norman's arrival in Pictou there had been a great disturbance in Mr. Ross's church with some of its members accusing others of witchcraft and demanding that they be prosecuted before the session. Mr. Ross laughed at them, and presently the commotion died. The same Mr. Ross had led in forming the West River Agricultural Society, also the first of its kind in Nova Scotia. He was the man, too, who relinquished to Norman his church at Middle River, when Norman, newly come to Pictou, had won away some of Mr. Ross's congregation and had no place to hold service.

Even by a man so co-operative, practical and popular, the introduction of a temperance movement into Nova Scotia brought opposition and ridicule. The very suggestion of not giving liquor to a man in your employ or to a friend who called at your house was considered a depth of meanness never previously heard of. To do, without rum, any work requiring a number of men was considered impossible. In a discussion on the subject a supporter of the new movement was asked what drink they would use, for example, at a barn raising. He innocently replied that buttermilk was a very nice drink. Of course, the new group was immediately known as "the Buttermilk Society."

There was soon a chance to test their principles. One of them had the frame of a barn to raise and needed a large gang of men. As usual, all the neighbours came, and all the temperance men from some distance around. The others, however, refused to help without liquor, and the temperance group declared that they could do the job without them. So, while the drinking crowd stretched lazily on the grass or perched in the best vantage points to watch the operation, the temperance men struggled and pushed. There were desperate "Yo-o-o heaves!"

but they could not raise the side. The spectators hooted and jeered, and finally strolled casually over to push it up. With a great show of vigour they finished the job, and then had their dram from the supply which they had privately brought.

It was only a year after the society was formed that there was a definite sign of progress. One of Norman's friends, Mr. Gordon of West River, put up the frame of a large house without rum. The substitutes were ale and beer, rather than buttermilk.

The impetus toward temperance was not only from the clergy. Judge John Marshall of Cape Breton was greatly disturbed by the increase of crime, and estimated that seven-eighths of the crimes with which he dealt were caused by drink. To increase the awareness of drunkenness and limit excessive drinking he led some religious and benevolent friends in forming a temperance society in Sydney in the early 1830s. Of this movement, Norman was a member and an active supporter. But, though he commended its work and associated himself with it, it was principally by his single-handed force that he achieved its aims in his own community. No doubt it was partly this success that earned Haliburton's approbation of St. Ann's: "Its inhabitants are Scotch dissenters, the most sober, industrious and orderly settlement on the island, and have a pastor of their own to whose exertions and vigilance the character of the people is not a little indebted."[14]

[14] Haliburton, Thomas Chandler, *A Historical and Statistical Account of Nova Scotia*, II, p. 228.

CHAPTER TWELVE

Farms, Fish and Timber

WHILE NORMAN was battling error in the Church, developing his school, holding in check his rivals in the community, guiding its spiritual life and maintaining by his own efforts the sober, industrious and orderly settlement, what was happening among the ninety-five per cent of his people who were not actively concerned with these struggles but merely accepted their results as the necessary conditions of their lives?

For most of them, the possession of land was the primary aim, a natural result of growing up in Scotland where the possession of a few acres could make the owner a man of importance in the kingdom even though only a small proportion of those acres might be productive arable land. It was also natural that pride in their possession should outweigh an understanding of its implications and responsibilities. As he visited Highland communities in Nova Scotia, Joseph Howe observed that the immigrants were likely to spend their money to buy more and more land rather than in cultivating and improving what they already owned.

It was not difficult to increase their holdings. Land was granted free to the settlers at least until 1827. One hundred acres were allowed to each master or mistress of a family and fifty acres for each child, the whole not to exceed five hundred acres. If the grant exceeded two hundred acres, the grantee paid five shillings for each fifty acres above the two-hundred-acre limit. In 1821, Boards of Land Commissioners were set up in various localities. To them the settler appealed for a temporary ticket of location, and when the time came to take permanent possession he was allowed to join with others, up to a limit of five, in one grant for an ordinary fee which was split among them. Thomas Crawley, who was in charge of land grants in Cape Breton, kept up this scheme there until 1832. The fee for one grant, listed in 1820, was less than two pounds.

Even at the beginning of 1839 it was estimated that half the population of Cape Breton were settled either without title or with only a licence of occupation. Many of them bought by private sale the land on which they were squatting. The price was less than three shillings an acre.

To become a large landowner in the new world was not an unreasonable dream, but for some the dream began too soon. Some of the Scottish agents had been glib in their promises of riches overseas. They pictured herds of wild cattle and sheep roaming about, free for the taking. Captains of the immigrant ships, too, were sometimes misleading about the length of the voyage, so that the immigrants came without provisions and had to buy food on board ship at such prices that they arrived destitute or even in debt.

Rev. John Stewart, who came as a missionary to West Bay in Inverness county in 1835, gave a dismal picture of the possible fate of these over-optimistic settlers. "Many of our people left their country without the means of paying their passage—the captain accepting their note of hand for payment when they could. A few years after their settlement, round comes the captain's agent for principal and interest. Money they cannot have—their cow is taken, or perhaps their land on which they have been toiling and the unhappy families must begin a new lot in the forest.... Merchants, too, very frequently cause this relapse into a state of abject poverty—the grant is taken in security for the value of articles provided. Many wants must occur before the first difficulties of settlement are got over.... Often does the bear take the cow intended to satisfy the creditor. The land must go, and hard labour with much deprivation be again resorted to...."

From such want and insecurity the well-organized settlement of St. Ann's was generally free. Money was scarce, the work was hard, and their precious crops and livestock were menaced by bad weather and wild animals, but the people were not unprepared. Those who had come by way of Pictou were acquainted with new world conditions. Those who came direct from Scotland were coming to join friends and neighbours because of their reports of the country. Unlike many other communities which might wait from ten to twenty years for a minister or a schoolmaster, they had teachers and minister with them from the beginning. The tremendous importance of these men lay not only in their spiritual and intellectual leadership, but also in the guidance in business affairs which Norman, the Munros, and several other men of the settlement were immediately prepared to give. In Norman's care even a confused and illiterate settler could be sure that his business with the land office would be honestly and efficiently handled, and that while there was money in the settlement, no hard-working man would be allowed to lose his cow or his land to any creditor from the outside. For such security in a strange land, many men would gladly sacrifice the freedom which they gave up to Norman.

However well his business might be looked after, the labour of surviving was a full-time burden to the newcomer. The forest pressed in upon him; his hatred of it dominates the Gaelic folk songs of the early years. "Tearing the tyrannous forest up from its roots," "Piling tree trunks on top of each other in bonfires has strained every muscle in my back"—even in the prosaic English translation the protest is strong. Confronted by the forest, he had no choice. Awkwardly at first, but with ever-increasing skill, the Highlander swung his axe and a space slowly opened before him.

He used the straightest logs for the walls of his one-room cabin, covered the rafters with the bark of the spruce and held the bark in place by poles fastened to each other and to the lower walls by ropes made of birch strippings. The family dragged to the cabin logs as large as the fireplace would hold. One of these would keep the fire steadily alive. With it, in a huge fireplace, they might use as much as a half cord of smaller wood in twenty-four hours. Often, in the winter night, as the wind searched out the chinks in the wall, someone was up to add fresh logs and keep the fire blazing. It was only a step from bed to fireplace. At most, each family had one bed for the father and mother. The children slept on dry straw beside the fire with plaids or blankets or only rags to wrap around them. When a passing stranger was storm-stayed for the night, extra straw was brought from the barn, and someone spared a blanket.

The fire was a lively thing, roaring and crackling, unlike the hazy smoke of the smouldering peats which they had known in their old home. There must have been a new vitality, too, in the gathering or "ceilidh" around it on a winter evening. They made up new songs to tell what had befallen them in Cape Breton. New folk tales, too, grew in a new country. Often they told of the night they visited the old wreck on the coast—a French ship it was, broken by centuries of wind and tide. Treasure was in it for him who dared to take it. Some of them had gone aboard to get iron for their own use. They came safely back. Then the treasure-seekers arrived. They climbed down into the broken hulk. Suddenly there was a flapping of sails, though the masts were gone. The wind whistled through the rigging that had long since broken away. Even in the bright circle of firelight they could still feel the eerie dread of their flight from the haunted ship, so that the simple crane made from its iron seemed almost sinister as it swung beside the fire.

So they talked and sang. The women had their knitting and, if the women were young, there would be young men to hold the wool for winding. Sometimes there was a fiddle with wistful tunes to take them back to the old land or gay rhythms to lilt them cheerily into the new. Dancing in Norman's land took place in secret.

The evening and the night passed by the fireside. By day the cooking went on there, in the iron pots hanging from the crane, or, for baking, placed in the hot embers. It was usually fish and potatoes that were in the pot, boiled together if the family had only one pot. Fish came fresh from the bay or was dried for winter use, and from the small cleared spaces on the farms, potatoes, for the first two years, were the only harvest. As soon as the trees had been cut, potatoes could be planted among the stumps, but the heavy work of prying out and uprooting the stumps had still to be done before grain could be grown. Even in the later years, meal was scarce, and the production of two barrels of meal in a year was considered good for an average farm. Most farmers also tried to grow a little wheat which was kept for special occasions.

Judge Marshall tells how in his judicial rounds he and his party unexpectedly stopped for dinner at a Cape Breton farm. His companions were immediately served with the family's potatoes and codfish, but the hostess did not consider this fare good enough for the judge. Instead, while he waited and hungrily sniffed the steaming food, she dried some wheat over the fire, ground it in the hand-grinder, sieved it, and made it into a scone which she baked on the coals. The buttered scone, with a precious egg, and tea was finally served to the hungry judge.

When the settlement began, tea was still a luxury among the Highlanders. From only a few decades earlier have come stories of Highland women receiving packages of tea as treats from sailor sons, and mistakenly cooking the dry black stuff and serving it as a vegetable. The familiarity with tea and the liking for it quickly increased until in 1847 John Munro was offering a reward in the *Cape Breton Spectator* for the recovery of forty pounds of tea stolen from his store. Both the theft, and the stocking of this quantity by the astute businessman, Munro, emphasize the popularity of tea. At its mid-century price of 2s. 8d. per lb., it would still be a luxury, worth stealing.

As soon as possible, each family bought a cow. If, as seems likely, a few cattle came with the St. Ann's settlers from Pictou, this good fortune would put them well in advance of their neighbours. Oxen would soon be available for the farm work, there would be some milk for the children of the settlement, and the women could make butter to go with the fish and potatoes. As well as the butter making, all the care of the cows was the women's business. Even in the new world it was many years before a Highland man would demean himself to work with them.

The crops were protected by the bristling rows of stakes known as the "dog leg fence," and outside the fences, from early spring till autumn, the cows were pastured in the woods. Often their calves were tethered near the house so that the cows would not wander away, but sometimes this method did not work. There is a story of a certain Donald whose cows failed to return. Late in the afternoon his wife went in search of them. When, after dark, no one had come home, the neighbours gathered with lighted torches to begin the search. Donald wondered about his cows which might have been attacked by bears, but as for his wife, "There's no fear of her. It's just a small island; she'll come out somewhere." All Donald's possessions were safely found. Others were less fortunate. Sometimes the animals were actually killed by the bears. In the late autumn there were perils for those who went in search—early blizzards in which an unwary traveller might lose his way and even perish only a few yards from safety, or treacherous ice not yet thick enough to bear his weight.

Since oxen were needed for the work of the farm, and cows for the supplies of milk and butter, the cattle were not grown primarily for slaughter. From Boularderie Rev. James Fraser reported in 1837 as evidence of a difficult year: "The people are chiefly confined this winter to animal food, being obliged from the scarcity of provender to slaughter their cattle, though by no means in a slaughtering condition, owing to the dryness of the summer. The crops of all descriptions were a total failure." Since game was no longer plentiful in Cape Breton by the 1820s, meat was seldom available in the early years of the settlement.

The tables on which the food was served were rough structures, hand-made with poor tools, but, however awkward its appearance, the family table was given the title of "the board." The family's gathering around it on the chairs and benches which they had made, for the food which they had won for themselves, made it a peculiar symbol of their self-respect and dignity. On one wall of the cabin was a shelf for the Bible, and beside another, a crude sideboard surmounted by shelves where the dishes were kept. It was known as the "dresser," since there the food was dressed to be served on the board. There was no other kitchen furniture in the cabin, but about a foot from the ceiling beams there ran a row of slender poles from which bags of grain and other articles were hung to dry.

Once dried, the grain was ground in the hand-grinder or quern which many of the housewives had brought with them from Scotland. There they had done their own milling to avoid the exorbitant charges of the landlord who controlled the local mill, and they had a special affection for their querns as symbols of their self-sufficiency. In the new country they were essential until, in the 1830s, John Munro and other businessmen built grist mills. Even then the home grinder was necessary. Ten miles of deep snow might separate a family from the mill. There are stories of men plodding this distance with 150 pounds of meal on their backs, and of a woman, when supplies were almost gone in the early spring, going to the mill and having to balance on a slender log across a turbulent stream with a barrel of meal strapped to her back.

Although progress on the farms was discouragingly slow, there came a time when most farmers expected to have, as well as their potatoes, a small crop of oats and wheat, with hay to store in their log barns. Buckwheat and turnips were later grown, and there were even a few experiments with Indian corn. Some of the more enterprising farmers planted apple or plum trees instead of relying only on the wild fruits.

Life could have been adequate, if not bountiful, if it had not been for the haunting uncertainty of the weather. Each year the entire year's work was threatened by the danger of early frost. The farmers could not plant their crops early, since spring was always delayed by the southward drift of the ice, so they were completely dependent on the good weather of the autumn for the maturing and ripening of the grain. Often those along the lake and the sea enjoyed more temperate weather than their neighbours on the backlands and might survive the first cold nights unscathed. But there were terrible winters, like that of 1832-33 when every kind of crop failed. Unripe potatoes and partly-filled husks of grain were the only farm produce to store for the long winter.

Then the St. Ann's settlers were fortunate to be fishermen as well as farmers. In the first years, when clear land was scarce, and later when blight and frost destroyed the crops, there was hope of survival while the sea was beside them and they were able to fish. Not only for the fishing but for the strengthening of their spirit, the sea was vital to the people of

St. Ann's. They could not be overwhelmed by the forest while they had their faces to the sea. Neither the isolation nor the scarcity seemed absolute, for the sea was not alien, it was a familiar part of their heritage, a way of communication, and, if need be, a way of escape.

Some of the settlers' problems communication could not solve. One of them was illness. It was almost impossible to get a doctor. There was usually an older woman who would come to her neighbours as a midwife or as a guide in the care of the sick, but she was sorely limited by her experience and her resources.

In medicine the resources were few. There were home cures, evolved through a long folk tradition. Mare's milk was a cure for whooping cough. Other diseases were treated with intricate compounds of the herbs which were grown from seed or discovered in the woods with the help of Indian neighbours. There were also faith-cures by the use of charms. Norman scorned such things, but the lore of centuries died hard. There was a charm for the toothache, and a charm for the eyes which would remove sties if it were recited by three people of the same first name. In cases of desperate illness when all the homely medicines had failed, a Highlander would find it hard not to try the magical touch of the seventh consecutive son in a family.

Faith in such magic, however, arose only from the need to do something when no other help was available. The settlers were eager for commercial remedies. Alexander Munro of Boularderie reported that, since he lived twenty-four miles from a doctor, he had given away to the people within a few days of his arrival the entire supply of medicines which he had brought for his own use. By mid-century, senna, the chief preventive medicine, was being bought in great quantities from John Munro's store at 3d. an ounce.

Illness was the greatest fear, clothing perhaps the greatest problem of the settler's household. In the strenuous farm life the scanty supply of clothing that they had brought with them soon wore out, and it was some time before they had wool from their own sheep or leather from the cattle that they could spare to kill. There might be a dress or a black suit brought from

Scotland and preserved for years of Sabbath and official wear, but clothing for hard daily use was another matter. The men, who must be out of doors in all weathers, necessarily had first call on the material for clothing. If necessary, the children could be kept indoors when it was very cold. At St. Ann's the school records show that the young children of poorer families were usually absent about one-third of the year. Even in 1840 Mrs. Munro of Boularderie was appealing to her patrons for cotton and flannel to make petticoats since many girls came in the winter to the academy with nothing but their frocks. Yet the academy students were usually from the most progressive and successful segment of the population.

When wool was available from their own sheep, the women of the household still had to comb, card and spin it, then weave it into the material for clothes or bedding. Shoes were an even harder problem. One of the Nova Scotian Gaelic bards warned his Scottish countrymen of what they might expect: "However good your trousers are, they'll do no good without two pairs of stockings and hair-lined moccasins that are tightly laced with thongs. It's the latest fashion with us to wear the hide, and all, just as it comes stripped from the beast the day before."[1] These shoes were made by hand from soft leather from the leg and knee of a freshly slaughtered cow. They smelled rather gamey, but they were ideal for wearing in the deep snow. Another type of shoe which they had worn in Scotland and still found comfortable in dry snow was called the "mogan." It was a sort of knitted slipper, strengthened with several layers of cloth sewed on to the sole. At first each household improvised its own footwear, but presently a cobbler settled among the other tradesmen in the community. By the middle of the century boots could also be bought at John Munro's store for one pound per pair.

Although all the women learned to spin and knit and mend, and many were weavers, only a few were skilled in making clothes. It was usual, instead, for an itinerant tailor to come to each home that could afford his work and stay a few days making up the cloth which was ready for him. Although wool was the only fabric which they could completely create themselves,

[1] Dunn, Charles, *Highland Settler*, p. 31.

cotton yarn was also purchased and woven. By the 1830s, blue cotton print, often with a white spot or sprig, was on hand in the stores for the women's dresses. Blue was also the favourite dye in men's homespun clothing. By the 1840s cloth of various colours, striped shirting, and shepherds' plaids, as well as moleskin at 5d. per yard, lining and trim for coats, glazed hats for 2s. 8d. and "ribands" for 8d. were all available at John Munro's store. Now family work was transformed into an industry and women were hired to card wool and weave for John Munro.

That the people of St. Ann's had a wider choice of manufactured articles than most of their neighbour communities they principally owed to the enterprises of John Munro. He began business in 1825, and a few years later, built his first ship, the *Isabella*, which he named in honour of his wife. He knew all the advantages of the carrying trade from his brother Alexander's experience in buying the *Ark* after its voyage of exploration from Pictou, and using it to bring livestock and materials from Pictou to St. Ann's. Now John, with his new schooner and the others which followed it, went into the timber business, buying timber and carrying it in his own ships to Liverpool, Aberdeen and Greenock, and receiving in return the goods for his store at St. Ann's. As many as seven large vessels loaded his timber at St. Ann's in a year. He also had other ships which were engaged in fishing off Labrador, and built up his export business in fish and fish oil.

For shipbuilding, black birch was ideal and abundant. Its wood was firm and close-grained, even more durable than oak, especially for the parts of the vessel lying under water. The trees, nine to twelve feet in girth, growing to a height of twenty to thirty feet before branching, made excellent timbers. In the building of ships the men were not immediately expert, but the principles of small boat building were familiar to the older men from their life in Scotland, and were passed on to the younger men who continued the fishing-farming life at St. Ann's. At Pictou, Sydney or Halifax an aspiring shipbuilder could observe the building of brigs and schooners. The shipbuilders grew from the need for ships, and so did the captains and crew. Norman could instruct in navigation, and in each season, eight or ten seamen, some of them from St. Ann's, conned the maps and charts in the navigation classes at the Boularderie Academy.

The money which John Munro paid to the men who sold, cut and hauled timber, or who built and sailed his ships, transformed the economy of St. Ann's. It placed within the people's reach a multiplicity of possessions and services, all available in the store or at the grist mills and lumber mills of John Munro. It made possible the building of comfortable homes to replace the one-roomed log cabins, and the buying of foods and materials which were formerly made at home. But it decreased the self-sufficiency of the community, and made it, in its economic dependence on one man, even more vulnerable than it was in the uncertain days of its beginning.

CHAPTER THIRTEEN

Famine

IN 1848 the settlement had existed for nearly twenty-eight years. Its business, educational and religious life were well established. The Cape Breton-born generation, at home in their environment, were now the young adults of the community. St. Ann's might have been expected to be at the strongest and liveliest stage in its development. The events of the year were to find it, at its very roots, dangerously vulnerable.

The story unfolds, month by month, in letters and documents. The first is dated March 18, 1848:

To His Excellency Major-General Sir John Harvey, K.C.B. and K.C.H., Lieut.-Governor of Nova Scotia and its dependencies etc. etc. in Council

The petition of the Rev'd Norman McLeod, and others, Inhabitants of St. Ann's

Humbly Sheweth

That it is from urgent necessity, bearing the evident marks of alarming destitution and threatening starvation around them, that your Excellency's petitioners feel themselves compelled to make this application for assistance, after the timely relief afforded to the country.

That petitioners have found themselves sadly aggrieved and disappointed by the unjustifiably inequal distribution of the said relief meal, fifty barrels only having been assigned to this widely extended district—bearing its correspondent proportion of late and poor emigrants—whereas the three adjacent settlements, namely: Boularderie, Baddeck and Middle River—whose combined number of destitute families can hardly overbalance that in this settlement alone—have respectively obtained a hundred barrels.

That petitioners attach no blame to your Excellency's generous intention and design on the subject, but to some of your mediums or advisers, who ought to have more correctly ascertained the comparative extent of the population and destitution of the respective settlements in the county; previously to their very responsible division of a relief on whose equitable distribution the immediate support of so many lives so seriously depended.

That owing to the grievously disproportioned division of the late relief, in reference to this district, several of its inhabitants, who might otherwise sustain their own households, without distraction, are sorely impoverished by the craving destitution of their neighbours, to whom the scanty assistance received generally served but for a very short time; since it was a half barrel of meal, which could be fairly allowed as the current quantity, for one here and there only, of the most destitute families; and such as were willing to depose that they did not possess the provision of a week for themselves.

That although the magistrates of this settlement have recently petitioned the Honble. Mr. Uniacke, on this subject, and warranted the payment of the requested supply, within a certain space of time, either in H. Road labour, or otherwise; yet that petitioners, on closer reflection, feel aware that there is a considerable number of their destitute families, which cannot be safely trusted to render any returns for assistance expected; so that without some relief of Indian meal, and seed oats, for them, exclusively of the quantity already applied for, by the said magistrates, they must be left to their fate, and unsupported, for, although disagreeable to relate, there are in this quarter, in spite of all example and reproof, though not so common as in other places through the Island, some people destitute, not only from inevitable circumstances, but likewise from more unthriftiness and offensive violence; who can well feed and flutter, dress and dandle, and carelessly chafe away with toddy and tobacco, whenever attainable—as a groaning burden upon economy and industry—and yet who must now or never be relieved from the very jaws of death, by Government—when their generous and soul-sickened neighbours can no longer assist them—with no redeeming pledge "either in lieu or labour, gear or gratitude."

That, on the foregoing mode of reasoning, it is earnestly solicited and expected that your Excellency may be pleased to refer to the prayer of the aforesaid petition, and to grant some supply of meal and oats, as above suggested, for the relief of those who must receive it all, either gratuitously or partly on very indulgent terms; and the same to be forwarded as early in spring as practicable; a favour without which, petitioners cannot now conceive how, not a few of their late settlers, and even several others of longer standing, can possibly be preserved from dismal suffering and starvation; as well as from serious trouble and danger to all around them, who already feel ominously alarmed for the fatal consequence.

The petition had ninety-seven signatures, among them the five magistrates of the settlement: John Munro, Ronald Ross, Roderick Ross, John Fraser, and John McLeod.

An outsider's view of the desperate situation at St. Ann's appeared the following month in the *Cape Breton Spectator*, as a letter from H. D. Sellon who had visited the district.

"The situation of the people here both in the Back and Front Settlements owing to the want of provisions and seed is really fearful. Not one person in every five hundred has seed of any kind to put in the ground and unless seed is, by some means, secured, the certainty of a general Famine next winter must be admitted on all hands. Not only has all the seed been used for the purpose of sustaining life, but cows, calves, and even the working cattle have been slaughtered for the same purpose. Many are now therefore without either cattle or sheep or the means of obtaining seed or food so that it is certain that if something is not instantly done, deaths from starvation will take place. Those who should see to it pass the matter by quite unconcernedly but they will awake to a sense of duty when human intervention will come too late. Why can not some of the Road money be appropriated to avert a famine and to save life? The Roads would not miss the sum so withdrawn for one year—and the emergency of the case demands that it should be done. Or why not take a few hundreds from those large salaried men who dress in purple and fine linen and fare sumptuously, who live by the labour of the poor? They can do with less for one year, or they themselves may have to share the fate of the starving poor sooner than they expect—for if Famine visit the land what will the maddened people care for troops or cannon or Death in any shape? I hear that two thousand pounds for the purchase of Seed has been granted—but of what avail is that? It will not purchase a bushel a piece for all who are in distress.

"Many that have provisions and property talk of removing to the States in the Fall, so that the little they have may not be plundered and devoured by the famishing population.

"If you think this will have any weight with those whose duty it is to attend to the state of the country, you will please give it a space in your well-conducted paper."

It was on June 1st that Norman wrote to his friend in Pictou: "The spring is very slow here this season, so that myself and my neighbours cannot leave home any sooner. The scarcity of provision, which has for some time been bordering on famine, throughout the Island, renders it inconvenient for some of our kind friends to leave their families; and they must fish, or do something else to provide for their daily support, to keep them from starvation. There never has been any thing like this in Cape Breton. There are several among us who could, without distraction, sustain their own families, if the burden of others around them had not fallen so grievously upon their charity; but the general destitution has made it impossible, even for the most saving, to shut their ears & eyes from the alarming claims and craving of those around them, running continually from door to door, with the ghastly features of death staring in their very faces; and especially since the expected relief from Government, for both food & seed, has been a mere disappointment."[1]

Norman made his visit to Pictou, and returned home with a gift of meal which helped to sustain the neighbourhood, until supplies were finally received from the United States. On August 22nd he wrote of it to Pictou: "Besides the relief of our own family, many a poor person frequented our house at that time, purposely for a meal, or a night's lodging, when they learned our having a supply of oat meal. In real truth I never

[1] Harvey, D. C., ed., *Letters of Rev. Norman McLeod*, p. 21.

observed so much need helped about our family by any other providence as the said supply. My dear partner could not but see the Lord's hand in it, not merely for ourselves, but also for a number of others from different quarters, running 'to & fro,' for a morsel to eat, or a platefull to carry home. Altho' at the same time, I have found it something very tender for myself, to be the medium of conveying such a gift home from my good friends. For it has in fact been the hardest task of my whole journey, and the greatest burden to my feelings. We have now the commencement of the new potatoes; but the blight has spread too far to promise but an inferior crop, even to the earliest planters in the Island; and late planting appears to be a complete failure. The other crops promised quite favourably before the present uncommon rain, which has continued already for a whole week, and is not yet over, by means of which the wheat, in particular, begins to rust, and thereby considerably to suffer. The Lord's hand is 'lifted up' in these steps of providence, tho' few consider his righteous intention & warning."[2]

For this distress, the obvious solution should have been in the enterprises of John Munro. Surely his purchases of timber and the wages of his workmen would have provided the money to buy supplies which could have been imported in the autumn before the dreadful winter, or at least could have been brought in after the spring break-up of the harbour ice. But John Munro did not solve the problem. The reason is partially given in the few issues now extant of the *Cape Breton Times & Spectator*.

First is a notice, dated June 2nd, 1849: "John Munro of St. Ann's, Merchant, having by deed of assignment bearing date First December, last past, transferred and conveyed to Messrs. Fairbanks & Allison, Merchants, Halifax, all his estates, debts, credits and effects—notice is hereby given that the said Deed is now in the hands of Hugh Munro & Daniel Munro (Sons of John)...and all persons indebted to the said estates are requested to make payments to the said Hugh and Daniel Munro."

In the same year there appeared in this newspaper a series of public letters to Norman from John Munro. One of them states Munro's position in the settlement's crisis. "I should nev-

[2] ibid., p. 23.

er have put pen to paper to take notice of anything you ever said against me—as no person cares or takes any notice of your sayings—they are taken as a matter of course merely—such as are situated within the circle of your authority must either sacrifice their freedom or prosperity in their secular affairs.... And although I felt annoyed, from time to time at your slander, still I never made an attempt to expose your conduct until I found that you had ruined my business—for hosts of people submit to your laws from circumstances and on the principle that those who live in Rome must act as Rome does.

"I spoke in my last of your obstructing us and harassing our energy while building our last ship. The gross manner in which you vilified us caused us to work at great disadvantage and this at the very time we were the actual means of keeping starvation out of the place! How glaring—how absurd must it appear to the eyes of the world to see a single individual assuming to himself the prerogative of prohibiting a starving community from buying food where they could obtain it in exchange for wood of all sizes and descriptions so as to suit the circumstances of the poorest. I trust your Reverence will take a retrospective view of the question and feel ashamed of your conduct—although that will not pay for the loss we sustained."

It seems incredible that in their starvation the people should have accepted Norman's authority in boycotting John Munro's store. The cause of his violent displeasure apparently was his belief that Munro was smuggling brandy into the settlement from the French island of St. Pierre. Munro states that the small quantities of brandy which he had received in partial exchange for his cargoes of cattle had been only for shipment to Halifax, and that when the Excise officers, informed by Norman, had searched his ship, they had found nothing. Roderick McInnis, replying to this letter on Norman's behalf, claims that not only did Munro bring "the only cargo of smuggled brandy and other contraband goods which ever troubled our peaceable harbour," but he also offered to supply smuggled liquor to another merchant in the county.

Whatever the precise details of the case, the notice of assignment is positive proof of the abasement of John Munro. It had been achieved, as usual with Norman's triumphs, in the most significant sphere of his rival's life. Wrongdoing had been punished, at the expense of hundreds of suffering people. There is even the ugly fact that Norman's sons were also engaged in the shipping business and that Norman is said to have owned a store. Could the people have been used as instruments of personal gain as well as of justice?

John Munro would quickly rise again, but even by forcing Munro's temporary failure Norman had proclaimed his power. In the name of morality he had made a starving people take a stand against the man who could have helped them. But by doing so he had made himself responsible, more completely than ever before, for a proud people who had been made to cry for charity and who found that they could be rendered helpless by the dangers which they had always challenged—dangers which a whim of the weather could bring again. For a leader of less faith the position would have been overwhelming. Even for Norman, nearly seventy years old, the new awareness of his all-embracing responsibility brought fears for his people's future, if not for his own. To Providence alone, he ascribed the sudden opening, at the height of their trouble, of a way of escape.

It was when the famine was at its worst that a letter and parcel from Australia arrived at St. Ann's. The letter to Norman was from his son Donald, unheard of since he and the *Maria* had docked in Britain eight years before. The parcel contained several copies of an Australian newspaper of which Donald had become an editor. For Norman there was great joy in the prodigal's letter and pride in his son's accomplishment as a writer. With rising interest, he and his friends read in the newspapers of the soil, the climate and the advantages of settlement in Australia. The young people were at once so excited by the letter and papers that, although Donald did not suggest their emigration, many immediately began to consider the British Government's offer of free passage to Australia from Britain.

Norman, too, was soon convinced that Australia would be a far more favourable country than Cape Breton for youth and young families, "if a cluster of friendly emigrants could gain the advantage of settling together near good sea ports & fishing grounds, with the advantages of agriculture & the salt water's refreshing breezes." Some of his children were interested at once, but for himself he thought very cautiously of migration. His age was a barrier; Mary, too, was over sixty and still in poor health. But against the physical difficulties of migration he began to place his fears for the religious opposition which might after his death overwhelm his family and friends if they remained in Cape Breton. For his people he could admit economic motives for leaving Cape Breton; in his own decision he would stress only his spiritual responsibility for the community. On these grounds he felt justified in finding divine direction in the new turn of events, as he explained to John Gordon, "I cannot...avoid thinking that the Lord may have some particular dispensation in reserve (thro') the circumstances of my dear son's random emigration to that distant, vastly extended, & unoccupied country; which is both mild & healthy, with many other advantages.... It is a point of very serious importance to a man of my responsible position what part of the Lord's vineyard in which my lot is properly appointed."[3]

So John Munro made his assignment, and in the Cape Breton newspaper the two factions waged the war that seemed to be tearing the settlement apart. But, thanks to Donald's timely reappearance, they were no longer confined within the limits of St. Ann's. Through the winter of 1848-49, as they waited for his response to their letters, they were looking outward again, receptive to a new hope in another new land.

[3] ibid., p. 24.

The schooner *Gazelle*, 175 tons, which brought passengers of the *Margaret* and the *Highland Lass* from Australia to Auckland, New Zealand, in 1853. Capt. Duncan McKenzie (photo next page) was master and half-owner of the ship.

Below:
Rev. Norman McLeod

Upper left: John Munro
Lower right: Capt. Duncan McKenzie

Oval pictures: Some of the first settlers at Waipu, New Zealand. Top to bottom: Duncan "Ban" MacKay; Mrs. Duncan "Ban" MacKay; Donald McDonald, J.P.; and Hector McKenzie.

New Zealand coast, looking towards Waipu. For the 1851 centennial, stone gates in the Waipu cemetery were erected by their descendants as "a memorial to the pioneers of Waipu who migrated from Nova Scotia and Scotland." The memorial reads: "These all died in faith...wherefore God is not ashamed to be called their God. *Fhuair iad so uile bàs ann an creidimh uime sin cha nàr le dia gu'n goirear an dia-san dheth.*"—Hebrews xi. 13-16.

Ebenezer McMillan, 1856 pioneer on the *Gertrude*, St. Ann's, Cape Breton, to Waipu, New Zealand. He is seated at the Waipu memorial to the six vessels that came from Cape Breton. Each face of the memorial represents one of the ships.

CHAPTER FOURTEEN

Southward to Destiny

IN THE SPRING of 1849 Donald's letter came. It was all that they could have wished. He praised the mildness and fruitfulness of his country. He weighed its open harbours against the icebound winters at St. Ann's, the invigorating dryness of its heat against the penetrating chill of the Cape Breton spring, the moderate winter against the frosts and blizzards. He urged even his delicate mother to attempt the voyage in the hope that the pleasant climate would improve her health.

His father, after the winter's reflections, declared himself ready to move to Donald's country, "if the Lord should spare my life, and pave my way for that purpose; and that for the concerns of both time & eternity; for which my motives are very numerous and various; and likewise dictated, I humbly trust, in submission to the will of Heaven."[1] The twelve thousand miles did not appall him, for, he wrote, "tho' the distance is long indeed, the direct course is over the mildest ocean in the world; for which reason it has long since been termed 'the Pacific,'" and "had we nothing in view beyond our own family, our children's coasting craft might freely carry us forward."

The migration fever had spread far beyond his own family. Donald's letter passed from hand to hand till it was worn to tatters. Little knots of people gathered to hear it read and to linger over it sentence by sentence. Families worried about it far into the night. It was not a decision for themselves alone. They were taking part in the breakup of the unity in which, through all its dissensions, lay the security of St. Ann's.

Inevitably each family had problems about its immediate relatives. Sometimes the wife's people were eager to go, but the husband's, well-established at St. Ann's, would ridicule the

[1] Harvey, D. C., ed., *Letters of Rev. Norman McLeod*, p. 26.

whole idea and argue fiercely for their side. There were family arguments, and there would be painful separations. But there was a greater problem that spring, as the rains and the days of surprising sunshine freed the harbour, as the bare branches were touched with green, and the soil lay black with a new year's promise. Was their security in the land that, despite its failures, was dear and familiar? In the homes that they had built, where their children had been born, where they had worked and dreamed? In the church and the school, in the graveyard on the side of the hill? And, for the far-seeing, in their new Victoria County about to be formed, a tangible part of the nation of which some men were already dreaming, the nation that in fewer than twenty years would be a reality?

Was this their security? Or did it rather lie in the unity of the settlement, the unity which Norman personified in his all-embracing authority, the unity which would go with its core to Australia. They had to ask of themselves one of two kinds of courage—the courage to break with the settlement's unity by staying at St. Ann's, or the courage to give up their homes, their associations, everything they had hoped to accomplish at St. Ann's, and set out on a twelve-thousand-mile voyage to pioneer once more in an unknown country.

It was easy to find economic reasons for leaving Cape Breton. Poor weather made the crops uncertain at best, and after the terrible year of 1848 they would always be haunted by the dread of famine. The timber business, too, had slumped. In Britain, their chief market, the reduction of duties on foreign timber, especially from the Baltic countries, meant strong competition for the Nova Scotia timber merchants. The shipowners had another setback when, in 1849, the British Navigation Acts were repealed, depriving the North American colonials of their special monopoly in the carrying trade with the British West Indies. It seemed, too, that the fishing industry might be endangered by the plans for a treaty of reciprocity with the United States which would give United States fishermen full rights to the inshore fisheries of British North America.

Anyone might agree that to leave was reasonable, but many challenged the need of going to the other side of the world.

There were other havens. In the year of the famine, several families had considered migration to the United States. Already a few young men had moved westward to Canada. Canada West was filling up rapidly, and as its farm production increased, experienced seamen and shipbuilders could be kept busy on the Great Lakes. There were opportunities, too, to settle on level, fertile farms in the moderate climate of the Great Lakes region.

Attractive though these opportunities might seem, they could only be for individuals. Australia with its wide unclaimed spaces and its comfortable climate could be a resting-place for the entire community, without disturbing their unity or their way of life.

Even for those who had almost decided that their security lay with the community wherever it might go, there were doubts and fears. The old people, who in their middle age had given up their life in Scotland, could look with nothing more than resignation toward another departure. To many of them, the move from Scotland had seemed a desperate, final act. Certainly, most of them had never seen Scotland again, but the ships of the colony crossed the Atlantic, and gradually the remoteness lessened. New settlers from the old Scottish neighbourhood came to Cape Breton; ships and seamen from Scotland visited their harbour; the ties remained sound and strong. As a barrier, the Atlantic had become familiar. There were no trade routes from Cape Breton to Australia; the separation would be complete. Those who felt that they must go would try by every means to take with them all their family and friends.

There was confusion at St. Ann's in those spring days. Some people dwelt on Donald's irresponsibility, his eight years' disappearance, and his gift of words. "Would you give up everything you have and go twelve thousand miles on the word of a fellow like that?" they asked. The others had been sustained through the whole winter by the hope of Donald's letter. They had searched out every possible fragment of information about Australia, and they were eager to be convinced. Donald's invitation was all they needed.

With stately logic Norman announced his conviction: "In

all temporal concerns we have not the least doubt that the change, if once compassed, would upon the whole be very far preferable to all honest & industrious people; especially among the mechanical & labouring classes. And as to religious matters, the case is not at all more gloomy than in our own country. Hundreds of families & friends might find indefinite localities for convenient neighbourhood, without any necessity of distant separation according to their attachment and manner of life.... All our best friends here are desirous of either accompanying or following us, if providence seconds their views; for otherwise I could never feel myself at freedom to abandon my sincere adherents; none of whom have any hesitation on the subject but how to get once clear of debts, & obtain a passage. I believe no people would answer better in South Australia than our Scotch people, reared in this country; and that there is no other quarter in the world which would agree more with their health & habits—especially those of them here in no exalted position in external situation—than the said colony, according to the detailed accounts we have, thro' various channels, of its advantageous circumstances.... If I should not so much for myself merely think any further & far removal, on my part, necessary, for the short remainder of my life, still I would think it on this ground, very reasonable & desirable, on account of both my children, and other young friends around us; and I do not know what more important duty I could fulfil for them, in the business of this life, than to assist & accompany them, from this now desperate & dreary place, to a kind of comparative Paradise—as my dear son phrases it—in our destined, tho' distant land to which I earnestly hope & desire the Lord in His time may be pleased to carry me, & a large cluster of our best neighbours, and other friendly acquaintances."[2]

For Norman, Australia had become the "destined land," and he would not delay. Before the end of June, 1849, his family and their helpers were at work on their ship, and he was explaining to John Gordon that he must delay his visit to Pictou because they had "a score of hands about our house at the work of our vessel," and his superintendence, especially in family

[2] ibid., p. 26.

worship, was indispensable. At that time he estimated that it would take at least a year before they could think of being ready for the voyage.

Under the charge of Neil and Roderick McGregor, master shipbuilders, the keel was laid at Black Cove, below the church and Norman's house. The builders were more practical than Norman with his thoughts of a "coasting craft," and among the practical men were the two principal financiers of the ship, John Fraser and John McKay. Fraser as a young native of Pictou had helped the settlers in their first years at St. Ann's; he had married the Squire's daughter, Mary, had become a respected citizen and a magistrate, and had judiciously sided with Norman in his action against his father-in-law. Now, a man over fifty years of age, he was ready, despite his secure position at St. Ann's, to begin again in another country. His friend, John McKay, had been born in Scotland in 1786. He had been sent by his father to Cape Breton to inquire about opportunities for settlement, and been so impressed that he remained and his family joined him at Middle River in the same year that Norman and his friends arrived at the neighbouring settlement of St. Ann's. "Red John" was well established in Cape Breton, but he was still an adventurous man who always rode a spirited horse and travelled at breakneck speed. Even though he was nearly sixty-five years old, he was ready for the new venture in Australia.

The ship made good progress in its first year. In Australia, Donald was kept informed by Hugh McKenzie, a teacher at St. Ann's who resumed their old friendship and wrote him in April 1850: "The building of the vessel intended to convey your friends thither is carried on with great dispatch. She is very strongly built, has an elegant model, and appears to be a first-rate 'clipper.' She has been completely planked and ceiled. The decks are laid and her outside is ready for caulking, so that she will, most likely, be launched some time in July or August next. She will be a barque of nearly 300 tons; but I cannot furnish you with her name now, as it has not been decided upon yet. Probably she may be called the *Margaret.*

"Your reverend father is fully determined on leaving Cape Breton for Australia as early in the next fall as possible, or, at least, before the navigation of this coast will be obstructed with ice, if he can by any means accomplish his intention.

"There is no doubt that the vessel will be ready for the intended long voyage before New Year, if rigging, etc., can be procured at a sufficiently early date for the purpose. There is one obstacle which will, perhaps, detain your friends longer than they wish. Their lands have not been sold nor is it very likely that they can dispose of them to any advantage; for the depression of the times and the great numbers of people that consequently go to the Canadas and elsewhere have greatly diminished prices and the value formerly set on landed property here. Therefore you may readily imagine the vast sacrifice of property which will naturally result from the removal of a good number of settlers from this limited place at once."[3]

Whatever sacrifices it might require, enthusiasm for the migration was spreading fast.

As soon as Norman's ship was planked, Neil McGregor left her in charge of his brother and went to the shipyards at the mouth of the Baddeck River to build a second ship for Australia, the *Highland Lass*. The McKenzie brothers of Baddeck, Duncan ("The Prince") and Murdoch ("The Captain") were eager to go and quick to invest in a profitable new opportunity by financing the ship.

About Norman's ship there was an eager bustle until the summer of 1850. Then everything stopped. All that the timber of St. Ann's could build had been done. The ship was well designed, expertly built, sheathed with galvanized iron. She was ready to launch, but there was no money to buy sails and rigging. Norman's property had been up for sale for nearly a year, but no buyer was in sight. Unless it could be sold for the money they needed, they would have to give up the enterprise.

Their enthusiasm for Australia did not falter for a moment. Rather, being prevented from the journey made them all the more eager to be off, and their goal all the more desirable. Some of the more optimistic members of the party had completed their plans to leave in 1850. They had disposed of their farms, since they did not expect to be there to harvest the year's

[3] McKenzie, N. R., *The Gael Fares Forth*, p. 47.

crop. They were packed up for a journey which might be this year, next year, or never.

It was an aimless year. They needed Norman's assurance that it was their destiny to go to Australia and that Providence would bring it to pass. Twice a week he led them in prayer meetings, praying for the money to rig the ship. Times were hard in Cape Breton; land was selling badly. What would lure any man to buy Norman's twelve hundred acres at the outpost of St. Ann's? The winter advanced, and still the money was not in sight. There were prayer meetings every night now. In the spring John Robertson came. He was a United Empire Loyalist who had prospered on the Nova Scotia mainland. For a sum equal to three thousand dollars in cash he bought Norman's property. It was all they needed—the money for the ship, and the tangible proof that Providence had intervened on their behalf and their enterprise was divinely approved.

As they worked on the ship at Black Cove, one of the most enthusiastic spectators was Norman's younger daughter. Peggy, the merry child who had delighted her father and the whole community, had grown to be Margaret now, twenty-two, vivacious and charming. Of course Norman's ship became the *Margaret.*

In the manning of the ship as well as in its name, Margaret had a special part. It began in the summer of 1850 when a barque from Aberdeen arrived at St. Ann's for a load of timber. The freeze-up was early that year, and the vessel was caught in the harbour ice. The officers and crew were there for the winter. Hugh Anderson, a young Aberdonian who was one of the officers, met Margaret McLeod, and they fell in love.

There on the stocks was Margaret's namesake, the ship which soon would carry off Margaret with her family to Australia. It was unlikely that Hugh's ship would ever take him there; it was even more unlikely that Margaret's father would sanction a marriage which would carry off his favourite child to Aberdeen. With their friends' help they made a plan. Hugh disappeared from his ship. The crew searched and enlisted the help of all the settlers along the shore, but he was not found. Finally in the spring the ship returned to Aberdeen, and the captain had to report to Hugh's parents that their son had been lost, probably through a crevasse in the harbour ice.

At St. Ann's the ship had been only a few days gone when Hugh reappeared as mysteriously as he had vanished. Rumour credited Margaret and her friends with hiding him in a deserted cabin and smuggling in his food. Now that he was openly in the settlement, he boldly approached Margaret's father and offered his help with the work of rigging the ship, and as a navigator on the voyage. He also declared himself a suitor for Margaret's hand. His work was immediately accepted; his proposal was ignored. But Hugh Anderson could be patient. He sailed as an officer of the ship, and, two years later, in New Zealand, married Margaret McLeod.

Even after the money had come for the rigging of the ship, the late spring delayed them. Until almost May the broken ice remained about the vessel so that the work could not go on. Their hope of an early departure faded again.

Some of the men who were waiting to sail on the *Margaret* were kept busy now about the ship. The others could find casual work from week to week, secure in the hope of a summer sailing. The women were busy preparing food to stand the tropical heat through which they would pass for months before they could replenish their supplies in Cape Town. Potatoes were shredded and evaporated and packed in birchbark wrappers. Dried codfish were also packed in the same way. As long as there was water to cook them, the familiar potatoes and fish could be quickly prepared. Meat was pickled, and, as the time of sailing came near, supplies of bread or a type of biscuit made without yeast were prepared. There were also experiments with the evaporation of milk.

The summer came and went. Now they were delayed by illness. It was probably the excitement and suspense of the preparations which brought a recurrence of Mary McLeod's ill health in the spring of that year. She spent the summer in a slow recovery of the strength of her body and mind. Even more serious was the illness of Mrs. John McKay, the wife of one of the original financiers of the vessel, who was threatened with the loss of her sight.

It was autumn and the woods of Cape Breton were red and gold through the dark pattern of the evergreens as they had been when the men of the *Ark* first saw the bay of St. Ann's thirty-two years before. The families bound for Australia began to pack their barrels, chests and boxes into the ship, and to distribute among their friends the treasures that they could not take. The *Margaret* was ready to sail. Conceived, designed, built and manned by the men of St. Ann's, she, like the *Ark*, would carry them on toward their destiny—this time on the other side of the world.

When he was ready to go, Norman formally ceded his church to the new Free Presbyterian Church of Nova Scotia. Although he had often abused the Free Churchmen and found them far short of his standard of excellence, he had in common with them their antagonism to the Established Church of Scotland. The church building was easily transferred, but it would be nearly five years before a minister could be found whom the people would accept in Norman's place.

It was not in the church, but on the open hillside above Black Cove that Norman preached his last sermon in Cape Breton. Even the large church could have held only a fraction of the crowd that gathered for the farewell. Below them waited the *Margaret*, trim and ready, surrounded by the little boats which had brought the people to the service. In the autumn sunshine the clearings across the bay were bright against the misty background of the hills. For the crowd that day there was nothing but the black-gowned figure below them, his white hair ruffled by the wind, his voice rising strong and harsh in admonition, breaking with emotion, gentle and clear in his final blessing. In those solemn moments all the diverse personal motives for the migration were absorbed into a greater motive; the removal was transformed into a pilgrimage, a tryst with destiny. Those who went were dedicated; those who stayed were comforted, but their spirits were challenged, too. Was there a destiny which they, as lone individuals, could achieve? Or was their future with the community wherever it might go?

They were losing the man who for thirty years had interpreted their destiny and guided them toward it. There could be no successor. No one else could unite in himself all the threads of the settlement's life. In that year their part of Cape Breton county had become the new county of Victoria and they had elected John Munro to represent them in the legislature of Nova Scotia. But his position was only political. Norman alone had the strength, the arrogance, and the sense of dedication to lead in every sphere of life. Many, as they listened, felt that the heart of their community was moving away from them. They knew that they must some day follow. The others who would never go would long cherish his strong gentle words of farewell. With singing and prayers and quiet weeping, the emigrants boarded their ship.

Suddenly the crowd was stirred by a flurry of excitement. John Fraser's daughter Mary was missing from the ship. The solemn farewells were suspended while her parents and the passengers searched for her. Then a sharp-eyed lad confessed that he had seen Mary slipping ashore half an hour before, and she and Hugh McKenzie, the teacher, were off toward Boularderie in a rig with a pair of fast horses. There was no doubt about where they were going. Mary and Hugh had been engaged before the migration scheme had begun, but when Mary's parents became promoters of the migration they would not hear of the marriage unless the young couple went with them to Australia. In his letters to Donald McLeod, Hugh had shown interest in Australia but he had refused to have anything to do with the migration. He was steady and cautious, and considered himself well established in Cape Breton. But he was also a determined man, and his determination included Mary Fraser. So now they were off, to be married by the minister on Boularderie, and they would succeed unless the Frasers could cut them off at the ferry. Mrs. Fraser commandeered another team and was off down the road after them. She was too late. They were across the Great Bras d'Or and on their way to the church. She reached the church door as the ceremony was completed. It was too late to interfere, so the Frasers forgave the runaways, and, six years later, welcomed them to New Zealand.

At last on October 28th, 1851, the *Margaret* began her long voyage. There were nearly one hundred and forty people aboard, including at least forty children. She was commanded by Captain Matson whose wife and children were passengers. Cabin passengers were Norman and his family; Roderick Ross and his wife, Norman's daughter Mary, and their children; Kenneth Dingwall, a tailor, who was Norman's factotum; Captain Matson's wife and family; Roderick McGregor, the shipbuilder, and his wife; and Donald Finlayson of Baddeck. Although John Fraser and John McKay were the original financiers of the ship their families did not travel in the cabin.

The *Margaret*'s departure had been solemn and dignified. The arrangements aboard were also formal. There were regular religious services and daily lessons for the children. Norman took daily observations of the sun and worked out the latitude and longitude in order to check the calculations of the officers. Most of the men aboard had some sailing experience and were allotted their share in the running of the ship. The women were kept busy with the preparation of meals. By all of them it was remembered as a happy time. They were freely on their way toward their long-awaited goal, and, aboard ship, the problems of beginning again at the end of the journey could still be held remote.

Off the Cape Breton coast they passed through a fierce storm, which was to give their friends at home weeks of anxiety about their fate. Once it had been safely passed, fair weather followed them all the way. The men in their shirt sleeves, the women in cotton dresses relaxed on deck, happily free of the tensions and worry of a Cape Breton winter. For hours the children watched the dolphins and the flying fish; they screamed with fear and excitement at their first sight of the gigantic albatross. Everyone crowded to the rail at the merest supposition of a sail breaking the horizon. Sails were very few along their course, but they grew accustomed to the isolation of their small world. They learned to cherish it. United in the goal to which they had held through all the doubt and impatience of their long-delayed departure, they were undisturbed by dissension and conflict. Having accepted the goal, even the strong ones felt it no sacrifice to accept Norman's leadership and to find his organization of their lives comfortable and even temporarily satisfying.

They called at the island of St. Jago in the Cape Verde Islands to send letters back to Cape Breton. Then on to Cape Town which they reached on February 19th. There the passengers spent a week ashore, and got fresh fruit, vegetables and meat after sixteen weeks on their shipboard diet. Eastward again for six weeks until on the port side there was land again—this time, their own land. There was little to see but the distant line of the shore, but they peered earnestly northward for any sign of what manner of place it might be. Although their telescopes revealed no inhabitants on the shores, they were no longer alone at sea. At Cape Town they had heard of the rich gold strikes near Melbourne, and they had seen there a few of the crowded ships that were speeding toward Australia. More and more were overtaking them on their route, or returning toward Europe for impatient prospectors.

It was on Saturday, April 10th, 1852 that they reached Spencer Gulf. It was an uninviting land, parched by an autumn drought. The young city of Adelaide, their destination, was several miles up the Torrens River. At the river's mouth the land was bare and deserted. It was too late to disembark that evening, and, on Sunday, too, Norman prohibited the work of disembarking and held a service of thanksgiving aboard the ship. Around them, the harbour teemed with fish, but since it was Sunday they were not allowed to catch any.

Although at first sight the land seemed inhospitable, they were confident of Donald's welcome in Adelaide. By now he must have chosen the site of their settlement. Soon they could begin to be at home in their new land. Instead they found at Adelaide only a message: Donald had gone to Melbourne. To some of the settlers this action must have seemed a disturbing echo of the old irresponsible Donald, to make them appraise suspiciously the land to which he had attracted them. But soon they must have realized that in a country where men were leaving farms and copper mines and every basic industry to flock to the gold diggings, an ambitious journalist could not remain behind.

They inquired about the possibilities of settlement and examined land in the vicinity of Adelaide, but the prospects were disappointing. There was nowhere the large block of land which they had anticipated for their transplanted community. They had hoped to transfer the pattern of living which they had established in Scotland and Cape Breton, with farming supplemented by fishing and their new Nova Scotian skill in shipbuilding. South Australia's coast had no hospitable bay, wooded and sheltered, and unclaimed, to be the centre of their life.

A few of the party, including the Fraser family, decided to remain at Adelaide. Within a few weeks, the rest sailed on to Melbourne, arriving there at the beginning of June. There, the satisfaction of meeting Donald was almost lost in their dismay at the city which they found. For the first time Norman had cause to doubt the providential wisdom of their move. Since news of the gold discovery had spread around the world, immigrants were pouring in at the rate of two thousand per week. This into a city which, the year before, had only 25,000 people. There were men of all classes and occupations from every country in Europe. There were Chinese, packed like cattle into their ships. There were disappointed survivors of the California gold rush who had made their way to Ballarat to try again.

Norman had struck another boom town, like Pictou which he had so often deplored, but a thousand times more frantic and lawless than the little Nova Scotian town had ever been. The people of the *Margaret* found shelter in Canvastown, two miles from the centre of the swarming city. Their money was gone. Money was essential in Melbourne where even a bucket of water, scarcely fit to drink, cost 2s. 6d. Their only resource was the *Margaret*. They sold her, and with her went their freedom to escape.

CHAPTER FIFTEEN

A New Home

MEANWHILE the *Margaret*'s sister ship, the *Highland Lass*, was on her way to Australia. Under Neil McGregor's direction her construction had gone steadily forward. There was no lack of money: her owners, Duncan and Murdoch McKenzie, were established storekeepers and ship-owners at Baddeck, creditors to a large section of their community.

Their *Highland Lass* was a brig of 179 tons, smaller than the *Margaret*, a graceful little ship, jauntily launched to the gay strains of the pipes. It was a late autumn day but winter had not yet threatened the shores of the Bras d'Or. When they took her for a trial cruise off the Baddeck shore, her fresh sails were free and beautiful against the chill blue of the lake and the dark outlines of the early winter woods. This was not the solemn mood of the *Margaret*'s preparation. There were cheers from the shore, for a bonnie ship and the people who would sail in her to a great adventure.

With the exception of the McKay family most of the *Margaret*'s passengers had been from St. Ann's. To the *Highland Lass* they came from many parts of Cape Breton, and even from Prince Edward Island. They were all friends of Norman and of the St. Ann's people; through them their enthusiasm had been stirred for the voyage, but only a few were of the closely knit community around St. Ann's Bay. Instead they were principally from Baddeck, with some from Middle River, Boularderie, and Big Harbour as well as St. Ann's, and single individuals from Sydney and Sydney Mines.

The passengers brought their chests and barrels to the shore, and the loading was quickly begun so that they might be on their way before Christmas. When everything was stowed away, they went aboard. The farewells were over; with the threat of winter adding an almost-welcome urgency they had hurried through the sadness of the last moments. Overnight came the snow, and the heavy frost. The ice began to close in around the ship, and they knew that they would not sail that winter. The adventurers straggled ashore. Some who had been unable to sell their homes could return to them; others went to stay with friends. The food that they had prepared for the voyage remained on board, preserved by the cold of the winter. For their winter's food, as well as for shelter, many of the waiting passengers had to depend on their friends. Their resources were all in their possessions aboard the ship and, when they had paid their passage, there was little money left to buy food.

By the beginning of May the ice was breaking up, and, early on Monday morning, May 17th, 1852, under the command of Captain Jordan of Halifax, the *Highland Lass* weighed anchor. Alexander Mackay, one of her passengers, described the first hours of her voyage. "Running down the channel between Boularderie Island and the mainland, no doubt to show off his trim little brig, Capt. Jordan set all sail, including studding sails. The wind was fair and all went well till near the end of the island. Here she suddenly met a head wind and, being awkward to handle with so much sail, she grounded and had to remain there until the flood tide lifted her off. She, however, got away before evening."[1]

The passengers, disturbed by the ill omens of delay, were cheered by the open sea. They had a fair voyage, but there were problems aboard ship. Only a few days after they left an epidemic of chickenpox broke out among the children. About a week later there was trouble with the food. Much of the ship's bread was found to be spoiled and had to be thrown overboard —with the disturbing knowledge that for nearly three months there would be no way to replenish the food for the 136 people aboard. They encountered heavy rains, a problem for their open fires, delaying the cooking of their meals for many hours, but a great boon to their water supply. They spread out sails to catch the rain and filled the casks with water, some of it fit to drink, the rest used for washing.

[1] McKenzie, N. R., *The Gael Fares Forth*, p. 52.

There was joy and tragedy. When they were about five weeks under way a baby was born. Only a few days later, one of the adventurous young men who was going alone to seek his fortune in Australia was lost overboard, and, before they reached the Cape of Good Hope, Hector McKenzie's wife died. She was buried at Simonstown, Cape of Good Hope, where they remained for three weeks. Both before and after their rest at the Cape there was considerable sickness among the passengers. It was probably the result of their sailing at the end of a long difficult winter, rather than, like the people of the *Margaret*, after a healthy summer out of doors.

The entire project differed from the *Margaret.* The routines of school lessons and religious services were not rigidly followed. Although the owners shared at times in the work of the ship the passengers felt no obligation to take part, and time was long for them. One of them, a young man named Roderick McKay, had taken courses in bookkeeping and navigation at the night school at Middle River, and decided to pass his time by keeping a logbook although he was not a member of the crew.

The McKenzie brothers were interested in the ambitious young man, and ordered that he should be given access to the ship's official logbook so that he could check his calculation with the captain's. Soon after they left, it was obvious that Captain Jordan was drinking heavily. McKay began to find some of the figures in the logbook unreliable, but said nothing about it and hoped that things might improve. Instead, some time after they had crossed the equator, he calculated that the ship was far off her proper course, and by his reckoning, could be running straight into danger. He checked and re-checked his calculations, hesitant from his inexperience to challenge an experienced captain, but finally he approached the owners of the ship. The McKenzies, both master mariners, immediately verified and approved his figures. They ordered that the ship's course be changed, and kept Captain Jordan under their supervision until the ship reached Simonstown. There they relieved him of his command and Captain Murdoch McKenzie himself took over for the voyage to Adelaide.

It was October 6th, 1852, when the *Highland Lass* arrived

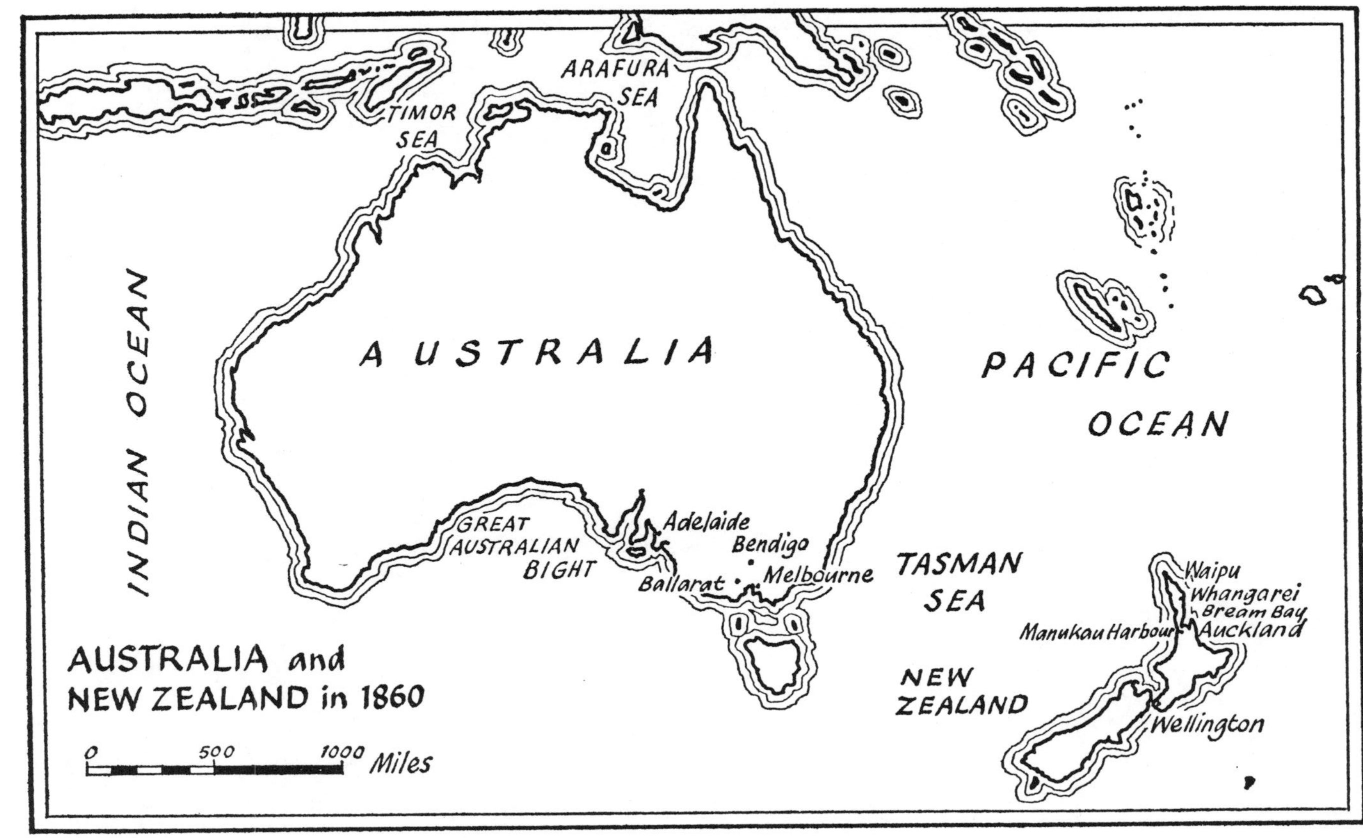
AUSTRALIA and
NEW ZEALAND in 1860
0 500 1000 Miles
INDIAN OCEAN
TIMOR SEA
ARAFURA SEA
AUSTRALIA
GREAT AUSTRALIAN BIGHT
Adelaide
Bendigo
Ballarat
Melbourne
TASMAN SEA
PACIFIC OCEAN
NEW ZEALAND
Waipu
Whangarei
Bream Bay
Manukau Harbour
Auckland
Wellington

in Adelaide. Through the tedious weeks of their voyage they had kept themselves cheered by talking of the ideal home which the people of the *Margaret* would have found for them. Instead they found only a few of their friends to welcome them and to explain what was happening to the rest.

What they heard from Melbourne did not raise their hope of anything better there. Even if it had, these people had paid their passage only to Adelaide, and the McKenzies had no reason to put their brig at the disposal of their passengers. They were anxious to use her at once in the carrying trade which had ready profits for their stout little ship and their experienced crew. The immigrants knew at once that Adelaide would not be their home but they remained there for nearly a year. Work was plentiful, jobs were developing with the growing town and were left empty by the men who had gone to find their fortune in the gold-fields. In reasonable comfort they waited.

Meanwhile in Melbourne the *Margaret* settlers had given up hope of finding land. Some of them joined the diggers at the gold-fields of Ballarat and Bendigo. The lucky ones found the gold that would later buy their farms. Others, less daring, used their skills to work at high wages as carpenters in the fast-growing city. Whatever they did they considered only temporary, an interlude until their scattered settlement should come together again.

One of their greatest fears was that the young people would wander into new interests and cease to identify themselves with the community. This, Norman felt it his duty to prevent. Wherever they went he visited them and kept them in touch with their people, although to visit a scattered congregation here meant dangers undreamed of in Cape Breton. Between the diggings and Melbourne the road was constantly threatened by bushrangers, highwaymen who lay in wait for the miners returning to town with the receipts for their gold, to be cashed at the Treasury in Melbourne. The bushrangers robbed or even killed the miners and collected the payment for the receipts.

On one of his journeys Norman was lost in the bush and accidentally came upon a party of these rogues. Out of respect for his calling, and probably also because he had little money, they spared his life and invited him to share their campfire for the night. Seizing the opportunity, he lectured them for hours on their evil ways. They were probably very glad to give him back his horse and send him on his way in the morning. Fearless, as he had always been, Norman continued to go where he would, undaunted by the peril and violence ever-present even in the streets of Melbourne. But a more subtle enemy was awaiting him.

As well as lawlessness, poor sanitary conditions necessarily accompanied the overcrowding of the town. The travellers must often have remembered the pure water sparkling over the rocks in Cape Breton and the cool fragrance of the pines beside St. Ann's Bay. Now the air was heavy with the stench of Canvastown, and water, scarce and expensive, was impure. It was only a few months until typhoid fever broke out. Within six weeks, Norman's three youngest sons were dead—Alexander, Samuel, and Edward, the eager, brilliant lad who was only twenty-two.

For the first time since he had assumed leadership, Norman knew bitter despair. He had supported the people with his own assurance of destiny when the *Frances Ann* was in peril on the Atlantic nearly forty years before; he had uprooted them from Pictou into the *Ark* and his destined community at St. Ann's. He had built himself into the heart of that community, and then, in the name of destiny, had removed himself and willed the community to go with him, twelve thousand miles to this perilous place. Had he acted in sinful pride? Were his three boys the price of his power? Had he brought his people here in search only of the kingdom of God, or of a richer temporal kingdom for his own glory?

Now, when he was seventy-two years old, Norman faced completely for the first time since his youth the possibility that the glory of Norman McLeod could be in conflict with the glory of God. From the time when he had accepted the fact of his divine calling, his ways and God's ways had always seemed the same. But had he, all these years, been mistaking his own voice for the voice of God? He looked at his own motives as ruthlessly as he had for so long scrutinized the motives of his fellow men.

There were weeks of doubt and despair, but his long habit of pride and courage kept him from surrender. Now, instead of imposing his strength upon his people, he himself was searching for strength and desperately summoning it to meet their needs—needs for which he must bear the responsibility. Responsibility saved him. Through pride and duty he came back to faith. Slowly he learned to accept for himself what he had preached to others, that there was purpose but not punishment in the death of his children. He rose again to the demands of his leadership, determined to delay no longer in finding the wholesome place to which, he must believe, destiny had called them.

They had been hearing many reports of New Zealand. At the beginning of the century there had been terrible tales—of ships wrecked on its coast and their crews captured and eaten by the natives, of white men being executed in formal tribal councils because they had unwittingly touched a sacred object, of the ruthless massacre of government surveyors and policemen. Only a few years before they left Cape Breton they had read in British newspapers of the settlers at Port Nicholson surrounding their settlements with earthworks and forming militia units for their own defence against the Maoris.

In 1846 the British Government had appointed as Governor of New Zealand Sir George Grey, formerly Governor of Australia, and the Australians were watching his administration with considerable interest. He was making great progress in the settlement of the disturbances, and was quickly gaining a reputation for general reform in the administration and conditions of land settlement. Under the improved conditions the land had soon become attractive to settlers, so that in five years the whole complexion of the country had changed. Now the growth of an agricultural colony was threatened by greater excitement in other parts of the world. Some settlers were lured by the gold rush in California; many more left their land to search for gold in Australia. New Zealand's need was so great that a reward of 500 pounds was offered to anyone who discovered a payable gold-field in the colony. Even with this lure no rich mines immediately appeared; it seemed that agriculture was to be the future of the young colony.

There lay its attraction for Norman and his friends. Even in Cape Breton they had heard of the Scottish colonizing expedition to Dunedin in 1847, and through Scotland had received good reports of it before their own departure. Everything suggested that group settlements were welcomed and encouraged. On the other hand, although Sir George Grey was steadily improving relations with the Maoris, there were still incidents of unrest and discontent over the disposal of land. Dangers of hostile natives were new to the people of St. Ann's. But the women said, "In Nova Scotia there was snow, in Australia there are snakes, and in New Zealand there's the Maoris. They'll be the least trouble."

Early in 1853 Norman wrote to Sir George Grey. He explained his people's need for a block of land and asked that a site might be reserved for them in the colony of New Zealand. To Sir George Grey they appeared the ideal type of settlers to establish roots in a new country. He immediately encouraged them to come.

Again their eyes brightened and their steps became brisk with the hope of a better place. They no longer had the *Margaret*, but since the previous autumn, the *Highland Lass* was in Australian waters. As long as part of the St. Ann's family had a ship, they could make a plan of migration. The McKenzie brothers were carrying on a profitable trade with the *Highland Lass*, but they agreed that Australia was not the home for their settlement, and planned to move their people once more. They sold the *Highland Lass* and, with the proceeds, bought the schooner *Gazelle* which they fitted up for passengers. She sailed from Adelaide on September 2nd, 1853, with ninety of the *Highland Lass* passengers and nineteen of the people from the *Margaret*, principally those who had remained in Adelaide the year before when the *Margaret* had continued to Melbourne. Neither Norman nor any of his family were passengers on this voyage.

Across the Tasman Sea, around the northern tip of North Island, down the east coast—fifteen days later the *Gazelle* docked in Auckland. Her coming caused no unusual stir in the busy harbour nor in the town that straggled up the hillside. There were tall barques from London bringing settlers, and schooners from the Australian ports loading their cargoes of flour and mutton. There were the tiny boats bringing potatoes and firewood and kauri gum from the coastal settlements into the growing town. Among them one more Australian schooner went almost unnoticed, but the local shipping reporter observed, as unusual facts, that the *Gazelle*'s captain, Murdoch McKenzie, had brought with him his wife and five children, and that in the passenger list, women outnumbered men. In the September 21 issue of the *New Zealander* was an announcement at the foot of the Shipping Intelligence column that "the schooner *Gazelle* has brought a number of immigrants who we trust will prove a valuable addition to the population—arriving as they have at a time when practical agriculturists are so much needed all over the district. They are originally from the north of Scotland, had first emigrated to America, from thence to South Australia, where they remained but a year and have been attracted to this country by its superior agricultural advantages for which it is becoming so deservedly famed."

At a time when many settlers were leaving for the Australian gold-fields, New Zealand naturally noted this small triumph over her flourishing neighbour. Then, to all outward appearances the *Gazelle* and her passengers merged into the routine of New Zealand life and it was left to them to establish and maintain their identity. They settled down in rented houses in Auckland to wait for their friends and for the decision about their grant of land. The *Gazelle*, after a month in harbour, made a short trading voyage around the north tip of the island. Returning to Auckland, she picked up a number of Australia-bound passengers and set sail for Melbourne on November 25th.

As soon as she docked Norman was ready to leave for Auckland, but there was a few weeks' delay while sufficient passengers were found to make the voyage worthwhile. In their eighteen months in Melbourne the people of the *Margaret* had scattered. Since there was abundant choice of jobs they went where the work suited them best, for in the tents and temporary shacks that were their homes there was nothing fixed or permanent. They felt that their life in Melbourne was transient, but they were not immediately ready to give up well-paid Australian jobs to wait in rented houses in Auckland for a suitable site for their settlement. So much independence they had learned, although they were still of the family. It was with a much smaller passenger list than on her previous voyage that the *Gazelle* sailed from Melbourne on January 7th, 1854. Norman, his wife, his daughter Margaret, his daughter Mary, her husband Roderick Ross and their children, and Norman's servant, Kenneth Dingwall, were all aboard. There were few other families on this voyage, and several of the individuals were not Nova Scotia migrants. It was a tedious journey, requiring nineteen days although they reduced the distance by more than three hundred miles by docking at Manukau Harbour on the west coast of North Island, across a six-mile neck of land from Auckland.

Meanwhile the first party of settlers had been appraising the country. As they had sailed along the eastern coast toward Auckland, their hearts had warmed to the familiar land. The forest-fringed shore, opening into deep quiet bays, rising gently toward the enclosing hills—it was Cape Breton again, but a mild and luxuriant Cape Breton. They remembered how the men of the *Ark* had told of their first sight of St. Ann's. With the same assurance the people of the *Gazelle* knew that this land would be their home.

Sir George Grey welcomed them and recommended that they settle in the Hawkes Bay district farther south along the eastern shore where the land was immediately available, or in the South Island where there were few Maoris to deal with and they could have a wide selection of land. Time would show that they might have been wise to accept these offers, but their heart was set on their chosen shore.

Captain Duncan McKenzie and a party of six men hired an open boat and went north to inspect the coast. They called at Mangawai to inspect the Tara block of about 3,500 acres which they found too small for their settlement. Then they entered the Waipu River. Conditions were favourable, and the shifting sandbar at the river's mouth which was to be a constant hazard did not interfere with their small boat. The land seemed as attractive as when they had seen it from the ship. They decided that this must be their site, and established the boundaries of the block which they would need.

Before the end of the year a notice appeared in the *Auckland Provincial Gazette*.

Commissioner of Crown Lands Office,
Auckland, November 26th, 1853.

The following person having applied for a defined Run, the description of the Run claimed now lies at this office, for the inspection of any person concerned.

Name of Applicant	*Description of Run*
Duncan McKenzie	Situated at Whangarie; bounded on the East by the Sea, on the North by the river or harbour of Whangarie, on the West by a branch of the same river, called "Hira Atata" and on the South by a range of hills commencing at the Bream Tail.

Edward Mayne,
Commissioner of Crown Lands.

The claim was soon challenged, by an advertisement in the *New Zealander*, December 24th, 1853:

CAUTION

Whereas a notice has appeared in the *Auckland Provincial Government Gazette*, No. 7, dated 20th December, 1853, which notice purports to be issued from the office of the Commissioner of Crown Lands, and dated 26th November, 1853, to the effect that Duncan McKenzie has applied for a defined run at Wangarei. And whereas all the land comprised within the boundaries specified in the same notice is my property, and no person has any lawful authority to interfere therewith without my permission, the said Duncan McKenzie and all other parties are hereby cautioned and warned not to interfere or intrude upon the said land.

James Busby.

Busby appeared to have a well-founded claim. He had bought the land from the Maoris in 1840 on the eve of his retirement as British Resident at the Bay of Islands. For more than one hundred thousand acres he had paid, according to his witness, Rev. William Colenso, "£40 in gold, 60 blankets, 10 coats, 10 trowsers blk., 25 ditto white, 20 shirts, 25 ditto white, 4 cloaks, 5 gown pieces, 15 handkerchiefs, 3 hakimana (single-barrelled guns), 20 hoes, 20 karauni (Dutch hoes), 20 patiti (hatchets), 15 iron pots, 20 adzes and axes, 2 bags shot, 5 canisters powder, 80 lbs. tobacco, 1 box pipes. Gift to Tirarau (the chief) 1 double-barrelled gun."[2]

Apparently the Maoris were satisfied by this payment, but the law provided that no one was to be awarded more than 2,560 acres without special permission from the government. Eventually, Busby's claims on Whangarei were disallowed, and most of the land in dispute was bought again from the Maoris by the government. At first the Maoris refused to accept the government's payment because they had already sold the land to Busby, but finally they agreed to be paid twice for the same land. From the government they received, in the period from February to May, 1854, £1,420 for three blocks of land in the district chosen by the Nova Scotians.

The completion of these arrangements was particularly delayed by the recall to England of Sir George Grey at the end of 1853 and his replacement by Lieut.-Colonel R. H. Wynyard, who had much less experience and influence with the Maoris. The colonists also found him less sympathetic to their particular need. Their problem was that they did not have enough capital to buy a block of land large enough to settle all who might follow them from Nova Scotia. They were willing to pay the set price of ten shillings an acre for the land they took up immediately, but they would do this only if an adjacent block were reserved for the others. With this plan Wynyard hesitated to agree, but finally it was established that Waipu should be set apart and reserved exclusively for the Nova Scotians.

The plans for the settlement could then proceed and on May 30th, 1854, the first purchase of land was made by Duncan McKay. He paid four hundred pounds sterling for eight hundred acres of land at Mangawai, Waipu, "at ten shillings per

[2] ibid., p. 247.

acre, five per cent for roads and five per cent for surveys being deducted." Until April 1856 the set price of ten shillings an acre for all rural land had to be paid in cash.

During these months, while Captain Duncan McKenzie was conducting their negotiations, assisted by Donald McLeod who had joined his friends in New Zealand, the settlers waited in Auckland. It was a congenial environment and they were welcomed by other Gaelic-speaking people. Norman held Gaelic services in a hall as well as preaching in English on some occasions in St. Andrew's Presbyterian Church. Although he was cordially received by the clergymen he still refused to form any official connection with the organized church.

Most of the men readily found work at farming or carpentering and their families mingled happily with the community. The young women were such a popular addition to the pioneer town that some of them married Auckland men and settled there. The settlers also formed a useful friendship with John Logan Campbell, an Edinburgh doctor who had settled in Auckland in 1840 and was prominently associated with the city for the rest of the century. He had a natural sympathy for his fellow Scots and a particular interest in these who had come in such a roundabout way from his native land. Some of them bought land from him at Whangarei Heads beside the block which the settlers had obtained from the government, and in some emergencies he loaned money to them without security. Also to Sir John Logan Campbell they owed their first school site, a section near the entrance to the Waipu River which he bought and presented to the settlement.

It was at the beginning of September, three months after the first purchase of land, that Captain Duncan McKenzie in his little seventeen-ton schooner, the *Don*, landed at Waipu three families—Duncan McKay's, Hector McKenzie's and William McKenzie's. In all, nine McKenzies and seven McKays, all former passengers on the *Highland Lass*. Norman McLeod went with them to the site of their new home, but he did not land. He left them with his blessing, and returned on the *Don* to his family at Auckland with whom he would presently follow them to Waipu.

Within the year, Norman's position had changed. He had followed the first settlers to Auckland; now he would follow the first settlers to Waipu. Perhaps if he had not been bowed down by grief he would have insisted on being one of the first arrivals in Auckland. Instead his son Donald had taken his part in the negotiations for the land. Almost by chance, the initiative in the migration had passed from the people of the *Margaret* to the people of the *Highland Lass*. The people of the *Highland Lass*, although they admired and supported Norman, were not chiefly of the close circle of St. Ann's which was the core of the old settlement. To them Norman was the minister, but he was not teacher, magistrate, major landowner, supervisor of their daily lives—the chief of the tribe—as he had been to the people of St. Ann's.

Because the community was a living force which created Norman as surely as he created it, he now remained the only thing that they still needed him to be—their spiritual leader. He went to give his blessing to the new settlement, but he did not stay to direct its work.

In a few months many more settlers followed to Waipu. Norman came then, with Mary who had found in the comradeship of the long journey and in the shared discouragements and sorrows a need for her restored strength. Of their three remaining sons, John and Murdoch came with them to Waipu; Donald, having seen his countrymen settled, returned with his wife to Australia and his newspaper. Their daughter Mary with her husband and children also continued to Waipu, but Margaret remained in Auckland, married to Captain Hugh Anderson.

The people who arrived at Waipu were not in every way the same as the people who had left Cape Breton on the *Margaret* and the *Highland Lass* three years before. Some had remained in Australia, others stayed in Auckland. Those who came together again at Waipu still felt the old bonds of the community, but they had found a new self-reliance in their survival through the years between. They were still content together and willing to share in the building of their community into another virgin land, but each family now lived with the knowledge that it had learned to survive alone.

In Cape Breton the rest of the community was waiting, unchanged. Now the word went back to them that the adventurers had chosen their home.

CHAPTER SIXTEEN

Six Brave Ships

IT WAS 1855. For more than three years the people of St. Ann's had been waiting for the final news. From the travellers they had heard of a world strange beyond their imagining, of disappointments, of movings hither and thither, of ways of life that they had never dreamed of. They wondered at some of the doings of their friends. At first they talked them over and tried to find reason in them. Later, accepting their remoteness, they accepted the news. The letters that began to come from Auckland were familiar, like a part of their own world. They felt at home with the news of the kindly Scottish people in the town, and with the wooded shore that their friends were waiting to claim, although they still might doubtfully shake their heads, remembering the fearsome stories of the Maoris. In the spring the letters came which cast the doubts aside and told them that the settlement at Waipu had been begun. The migration fever, held in check through years of waiting, broke out again.

In the previous year, John Munro, who had quickly recouped his crippling losses, had bought the brig *Gertrude*. She almost fell into his hands. On her first voyage from Prince Edward Island, where she was built, she was lashed by a severe storm, and left stranded and dismasted near the entrance to St. Ann's harbour. A well-built 215-ton brig where only he could conveniently salvage her was an investment that John Munro could not miss. He had her repaired and re-conditioned, probably even then thinking of her as a possible ship for the voyage to Australia. When the news of the New Zealand settlement reached St. Ann's, he determined at once to fit her for a voyage to New Zealand.

After Munro's bitter feud with Norman, who to the St. Ann's people would still be the centre of the New Zealand settlement, it seems unlikely that he should have planned to migrate. Probably he outfitted the ship only as a commercial venture, to transport a load of colonists and be sold in New Zealand. He must still have intended to remain when he contested the Victoria county seat in the election of May 1856. He was defeated, and by June 25th he had settled his business at St. Ann's and was sailing with his family among the 190 passengers of the *Gertrude*.

By the time of his departure Munro would have heard of the large part which the McKenzie brothers had taken in the business of the settlement, and would know that their initiative had been accepted by Norman. The McKenzies were men of his own kind, public-spirited businessmen, who would use their ability for the community, but would use it on their own terms. They, no more than he, would endure boycotts by Norman McLeod. In their accepted prominence there was an assurance that Norman was relaxing his hold on the business of the settlement, and there seemed little danger that at the age of seventy-six he would resume the all-inclusive authority that he had wielded at St. Ann's. Munro had also found in his years in the provincial government a special resource against any petty tyranny which Norman might attempt. He was assured now that even in newly-settled countries the days of self-governing self-contained communities were almost past, and as part of the centralized authority he was a part of the power of the future. But also in making this move Munro was a man of St. Ann's, a part of the family. He belonged to it, and in it even his far-spread business had its roots. Almost all his ship's passengers were from St. Ann's. His business was moving away; John Munro would follow it, even twelve thousand miles.

He hired Captain Alex Rose to command the *Gertrude*. They followed the usual course, tedious because of light variable winds, reached Simonstown on September 10th, remained a month there and arrived in Auckland on December 22nd. The *Southern Cross* of December 23rd reported that there had been two deaths and three births during the voyage, and that there had been little sickness on board until the last two weeks when symptoms of scurvy developed. It concluded, "It is fortunate, with so large an arrival of passengers, that they do not come to our shores friendless, but to meet their relatives who arrived by the *Gazelle*, several of whom went aboard to welcome them." The welcome and the home waiting at the end of the long voyage made the ways of the *Gertrude*'s people very different from those before. They whose lives had changed little in the years of their separation felt that they were only rejoining their old community, and by their feeling made it so. The individuals who in their years of migration had learned to be alone found in the newcomers the closely-welded group which they had momentarily forgotten. They again had a body to which they could belong and with the restored tightness of the community there could rise again the power of Norman at its heart.

Perhaps John Munro had anticipated this feeling; undoubtedly he was also concerned for the community's land and his own future property. Whatever his motives, he had taken steps well in advance to ensure his position in the community. Before leaving Cape Breton he had heard that James Busby was again challenging the rights of the New Zealand settlers to their lands, and that the government had still incompletely solved the problem. With the skill which earned him the nick-name "the Diplomatist," Munro, while in Cape Town, interviewed Sir George Grey, former Governor of New Zealand, who was now Governor of South Africa. From him he obtained a promise in writing that if the Nova Scotians were not satisfied in New Zealand they would be welcome in South Africa.

With this threat in hand he interviewed Governor Gore Brown in Auckland on his arrival, and was referred to the Auckland Provincial Superintendent. The Superintendent explained that he could not carry out his land policy because of lack of co-operation from the Council and suggested that Munro should contest a vacant seat in the Council. This he did, and was presently elected representative for the Northern Division. As a successful diplomat John Munro rejoined the New Zealand family.

Before the *Gertrude* left, her passengers knew that Duncan and Angus Matheson, two young men from Baddeck, were planning to follow them to New Zealand in their brigantine, the

Spray. She was a tiny ship of 106 tons, no larger than an average coasting craft, built and owned by the Matheson brothers. They had tried her out on the mail service between Halifax and Bermuda, and with no thought of her small size or the vast distance before them, they were ready to make the voyage to New Zealand. Angus had served as her captain on the Bermuda trip, and earlier had been captain of a brig which sailed from Halifax to Quebec. He was experienced in navigation and both he and Duncan had sailed for several years in the fogs and storms of the North Atlantic. They felt no dread of the long voyage, which, for the ships before them, had been relatively calm.

They were both young. Angus was thirty years old and was moving his wife and child with him to New Zealand; Duncan was a thirty-two-year-old bachelor. Their daring and enthusiasm attracted young people; bachelors and young couples with small children made up most of their passenger list. Even careful Hugh McKenzie who had made the runaway marriage with Mary Fraser five years before, changed his mind, and was on board with Mary and their three children. There were ninety-three of them crowded on the little ship when she sailed from Big Bras d'Or on January 10th, 1857, just in time to avoid being frozen in. The brothers had employed J. Duncan as captain and Angus served as first officer, though virtually as master.

The *Southern Cross* on June 19th, 1857, reports: "The *Spray*, brigantine, of Halifax, Nova Scotia, Captain Duncan, from Cape Breton, with ninety-three passengers on board for this port, 156 days from Nova Scotia and 11 from Twofold Bay, put into the Bay of Islands on Wednesday, windbound. No sickness on board, nor any vessel spoken."

What the report does not tell is that there were now ninety-six passengers since on the crowded little ship four women had borne their children and one baby had died. It does not tell that Twofold Bay in New South Wales was far off their course, and that the *Spray* had been driven to the Australian coast by a terrific storm which only a stout ship could have survived. A passenger described how the bowsprit "snapped like a pipe-shank" at the cathead. In the rough sea the wreckage was crashing against the hull. Somehow it had to be cut away. Although his wife and children were with him, Kenneth McKenzie was the skilful, reckless sailor who volunteered to be lowered over the side. Dangling from the plunging ship, he cut away the gear that held the bowsprit. The ship was saved, and the daring Kenneth lived to become one of the most successful smuggling sea captains of New Zealand.

The Matheson brothers sold their ship in Auckland, and in a month after her arrival she was sailing to Sydney under the command of Captain Hugh Anderson. The Mathesons searched for an ideal site for shipbuilding, impossible in the uncertain waters at the mouth of the Waipu River. They found it at Omaha, halfway between Auckland and the main settlement at Waipu, and took up land on the inlet that would be known as Matheson's Bay. Soon they were building ships again, with frames of pohutukawa, and planks and spars of the giant kauri trees.

Before 1857 had ended, a fifth ship was ready for the journey. With the news of the ready sale of the Nova Scotian ships in New Zealand, the fitting of a ship for New Zealand had become an attractive investment. Charles Campbell of Baddeck, the owner of the barque *Breadalbane*, had no intention of moving with his ship to New Zealand. She became the first of the migration to make the voyage under the sole command of her captain.

With the exception of a few from St. Ann's and Big Harbour, most of the *Breadalbane*'s passengers were from Boularderie, of the congregation of the Rev. James Fraser who had strongly opposed Norman's views. They were not sailing to rejoin a lost leader, but in response to the enthusiasm of their friends who had moved to New Zealand. So their journey was not a pilgrimage but a hopeful expedition toward a more prosperous life. Under Captain James, the *Breadalbane* was a cheerful ship with which its passengers, years after, still associated the rollicking sea shanty, "Our ship's a blue-nose clipper" that the sailors sang on board.

Of this voyage a daily record was kept by one of the young passengers, Murdoch Fraser. His diary for the first sixty days of the voyage from December 24th, 1857, chronicles the excitements and opinions of a young man sharing in a great adventure. There was Christmas Day when they "stood on deck ankle deep in snowy mud and the wind blowing hard with an incessant sharpness," waiting for their pilot to come aboard. There was December 27th, the first day out, when "it was cold through the day and many of the passengers seasick"; December 29th... "a heavy roll of the ship broke loose the lashings of one of the fireplaces, which smashed some pots and kettles and everything that was loose rolled about in a very comical manner..."; December 30th... "warm enough to stand on deck in our shirt sleeves, I seen a few of the passengers coming on deck barefooted..."; December 31st... "the brick in the lee fireplace fell down altogether and the sea washed all over the decks, and the ocean all around us white as snow, it was truly awful to contemplate the scene..."; January 1st... "a heavy sea broke in and gave us a thorough good ducking. I was almost all the afternoon hanging in the rigging to dry myself.... Considering the circumstances, we enjoyed our New Year pretty well, and I've seen some aboard quite funny, however everything passed off pleasantly..."; January 3rd... "It being Sunday all the passengers on deck looked clean and nice, and the most engaged in reading.... It is very curious the feeling which comes over us, on board of a ship on Sunday, till we get accustomed to it, when we hear the cry of the sailors, raised up, keeping time with their labour, we almost forget it is Sunday, and sometimes we actually but unintentionally commit ourselves but presently we shudder at our carelessness."

Even for the optimistic young man everything was not perfect. "Our family had no great reason to complain," he wrote, "all the complaint they could make was against that gold-loving cold-hearted villain who huddled and packed them into his ship close enough to be compared to a slaver, regardless either of our bodily comfort or of our valuable lives, or of anything that would tend to our well being. What but a heartless, souless and a heartless wretch like himself would be cruel enough to pack 32 souls in a space small enough to contain 6 persons, and half of that room stowed up with part of their luggage, and the rest exposed to all kinds of weather and the mercy of the waves. Our Capt. true enough is a very nice man, but his niceness is only a poor substitute in place of our health, wealth and all."

Captain James had many skills. On the fourth day out he set up regulations for the running of the ship, regarding such things as the lighting of fires, and appointed four men as constables, two as justices of the peace, and two to positions labelled A.A.L. He set the water allowance at half a gallon per passenger per day measured out by the mate. (The young diarist considered this quantity insufficient.) The captain was the principal mason in the rebuilding of the fireplace. He attentively cared for the sick. He and one of the passengers even had hens aboard, kept in a pen in the stern. Their eggs would be treats for a few fortunate people, but they would do little to allay the food problem. On the twentieth day out Murdoch writes that "the potatoes we took with us began to rot in heaps. A good many, good and bad, were thrown overboard; also I have seen some meat thrown overboard, on account of its being pickled with salt water which made it rot in a short time."

Murdoch, after four weeks at sea, had advice for emigrants. He recommended strong material in clothing, preferably moleskin or strong duck pants and shirts of flannel, since flannel is a bad conductor of heat. In food he advised rice as a light diet, and chocolate and coffee as drinks. He also observed: "Our bread made at home previous to sailing will preserve an incredible long time. It must be kneaded quite thin and nothing used in baking it but water"—"Potatoes should not be used for they are a regular nuisance aboard ship"—"If the immigrant intends to take any vegetables...let him take a small quantity of various sorts such as cabbage, carrots, turnips, beets, etc., all pickled in different strong crocks well covered, and kept in a rough strong box, but any evil disposed persons be aboard as in our case, he must watch his effects pretty close, or he will run the risk of having them destroyed as well as consumed."

The picture of a happy family expedition does not stand up under Murdoch's candid scrutiny: "To the shame of some of the passengers I have noticed some acts taking place between them which is no doubt an evil very predominant in society especially among some classes of people which formerly lived in different localities. When they associate together one troublesome person among a hundred will very often create a disturbance, especially by throwing a party's country, locality, sect, etc. into his face. Some parties will put up with this, but in general, the most will not. Aboard of a ship, where idleness is the general occupation, a disturbance is very easily raised, and should the disturbance be raised by children as it most generally is, men must set it right." The followers of Norman and of the rival minister of Boularderie would easily continue their leaders' feuds in the crowded idleness of their shipboard life.

For the physical ills of the travellers, Murdoch generously recommended concoctions of gin and brandy. Probably these beverages were more familiar to Murdoch in his home on Boularderie than to those who had grown up under Norman's shadow at St. Ann's. Murdoch also recommends care in the hot climates, against settlers' exposing their heads to the sun and the moon, and requires straw hats for both sexes with paper inside the crown. "We had some persons aboard," he says, "who were very sick from that cause and especially by sleeping with their faces toward the moon." They found remedies for the minor ills, but a laconic comment suggests the dread which must have filled the ship on the night of February 7th: "About noon one of the passengers was taken very sick by a pain near his kidneys, something like the cholera. He was bled and drugged but found no relief until about daylight the next day."

Murdoch writes of the winds and a violent storm, of the navigation of the ship, of excitements like the catching of an albatross that "weighed 20 1/2 lbs (alive)," of the whales, of dolphins and flying fish. There is a feeling of absolute completeness in the little world of the ship, but in a moment it can be shattered—"We espied two ships through the day, one of them went past to windward. About noon we seen the other one right ahead and coming in our direction. The Capt. cast the lashing of his gig to board her. Some began with lightning speed to scribble some words on paper to send to their friends, and some who would like to do the same, in their hurry could not do it, so that when the boat shove off some were seen on deck with late letters in their hands. When pretty near abreast the two ships hove to, the mate went aboard, carrying letters for Boularderie and...for St. Ann's. She proved to be a British brig from

Bounes Ayres, bound to Foy, West of England, but the Capt. promised to post our letters in England."

On May 22nd, the *Breadalbane*'s passengers rejoined the larger world. The *New Zealander* reported her arrival with 160 "hale, hearty and stalwart" souls. All of the ships had proved themselves on their voyage from Nova Scotia to New Zealand, but to the reporter the *Breadalbane* was especially exciting—"a beautiful vessel of 224 tons register, three years old, built of hacmatac for the China trade. Her model is perfect, and her lines exceedingly symmetrical, and we much mistake when in trim, if she be not a thorough clipper." She was not left long at anchor after her five months' voyage. Within six days she had disembarked her passengers, had been purchased by an Auckland shipping company, and was off to sea again.

Meanwhile at St. Ann's, life was resuming a new pattern. Five years after Norman's departure the people had finally agreed to accept another minister in his place. They chose Abraham MacIntosh, a native Cape Bretoner who had been trained at the Free Church Academy in Halifax. For two years he boarded with the Robertsons in Norman's old home at Black Cove, and, by the end of 1858, was sufficiently secure in his position to buy a farm at South Gut and build a home of his own.

With Mr. MacIntosh's establishment at St. Ann's the end of the old times had come. Norman's property, his school and his church were occupied, but there were people in whose hearts the vacancy still remained. Some were happy in the new order, others accepted it and learned to be content, but still others realized that for them there could be no substitute for their old community.

A group of them called on William Ross to inquire what his terms would be for passage to New Zealand in the barque *Ellen Lewis* of which he was a principal shareholder. He set the fare at sixteen pounds for each person with each providing his own provisions, and stipulated that the 336-ton barque should accommodate two hundred passengers. They easily found that number. Reports of the mild climate, the good land and the profitable shipping trade were coming back from the New Zealand settlers. Their friends and their old neighbours were easily tempted to move to a richer country. Loneliness was no longer a deterrent, for, among the hundreds of people who had gone before them, most people of the district now had as many friends as in their native Cape Breton. From Broad Cove, Baddeck, Boularderie, Middle River, Lake Ainslie and Big Harbour, they joined the people of St. Ann's until finally 235 colonists had paid for their passage. The rates were probably higher on the *Ellen Lewis* than on any of the previous ships, but most of these people could afford to pay them. They were fairly prosperous, they were going direct to their new land, and since April, 1856, land in New Zealand could be bought on credit, with only one-fifteenth of the price required at the time of purchase.

In December, 1859, the *Ellen Lewis* sailed from St. Ann's Harbour, and on May 14th, 1860, the final sector joined the colony. Other individuals would find their way to Waipu and Whangarei from Cape Breton and even from the old parish of Assynt. There would be some who would wish themselves back in St. Ann's and those in St. Ann's who would gladly have gone. From this day the going and the longing must be done alone. The great division was over; the six brave ships had taken their share of St. Ann's.

CHAPTER SEVENTEEN

Into the World

THE OLD COMMUNITY was in its new setting. In spirit it was still one large family, with its individual members strengthened and matured by the experience of migration. Just as the spirit of the community could be transplanted and would continue to grow in a new land, so in some ways its economic life could continue from its point of achievement at St. Ann's. But in many things the Nova Scotians began again from the beginning.

It was a dense semi-tropical forest which faced them now. Beneath the gigantic kauri trees was the thick undergrowth of the persistent ti-trees and the ubiquitous ferns which stood at shoulder height. Even in the winter the ferns did not die down, and only constant cutting could keep them from regaining possession of the land. Clearing was a community undertaking, as it had been in Cape Breton, with neighbours gathering in the bush for a working bee, still known by its Cape Breton name of "frolic." It was a two-part task—the boys with slashers cutting the luxuriant growth of the forest floor, the men with their axes felling the tall trees. Among the stumps they sowed the grass seed which grew quickly in the warm climate and soon provided good pasture. Even the seeds of the dry grass which came in their mattresses and packing-cases from Nova Scotia and was casually thrown out on the ground, quickly germinated, and the "Nova Scotia brown-top" became a speciality of the settlement.

The familiar wheat and potatoes were soon being grown, with the corn, pumpkins and melons which would flourish in the mild climate. The loose-textured soil, enriched by the ashes of the burned trees, could be prepared by a light working with a hoe. In the fine weather of the first few winters it was actually possible to burn off their land as late as June, sow wheat in the ashes, and harvest a remarkable crop. Within three years after the first settlers had arrived, a fairly large quantity of wheat from Waipu was being marketed in Auckland.

Auckland was beginning to develop a profitable export trade with Australia where the overwhelming growth in population meant a sure market and a high price for all staple foods. In the years from 1853 to 1855 many prices of farm produce doubled and some products, such as potatoes, tripled in price. A hopeful time for a new farming settlement, even though for their first livestock they might have to pay five times the price they had received for the cattle they had sold in Cape Breton.

There was an assured living for farmers in a mild climate and a good market, but some of the new settlers still feared for their lives. They peered apprehensively into the forest, alert for the ominous Maoris. In their district, relations between the Maoris and the government officials had been good, and the harshness of their customs had been softened by the influence of able missionaries. Still some settlers, tense with fear, were thrown into temporary panic by an innocent old Maori fisherman suddenly appearing from the bush, or a group of thirsty Maori hunters stopping at their house for a drink of water. One of the settlers armed his seven sons and fortified his house. He made a trapdoor in the floor and began a tunnel from the house to a nearby river bank. He also accumulated explosives and detailed one of the sons to blow up the house and cover the family's retreat through the tunnel when the desperate attack should come. None of the precautions was ever required.

Instead, from their knowledge of the forest plants and the pests which beset their crops, the Maoris contributed generously to their new neighbours. One of their skills, copied by some of the newcomers, was their method of building temporary huts. Roof and walls were made of palm fronds, so skilfully interlaced that from the inside they looked like a woven fabric. The settlers learned, too, to use raupo, a type of bulrush, for the roofing of their log cabins.

Their cabins did not follow the Cape Breton design. Instead the framework was made of large logs, and the walls of board-like slabs cut from split logs and nailed to the frame in a vertical position. A paling or a smaller slab was placed to overlap the edges of the larger slabs and make the walls weatherproof. The enormous chimney which towered above the roof was either made of wood and lined with clay or made of clay and supported by small logs. A few small, cherished pieces of the furniture had come with them from Nova Scotia; the rest was homemade in New Zealand. Most of the blankets, linens and utensils were from Nova Scotia.

The food which boiled in the iron pots or fried on the coals had changed only a little from their diet at St. Ann's. The porridge was now made of corn or wheat since oatmeal had to be imported. There was fish, and meat from one of their own cattle which they killed and cured at the beginning of the winter. The hunters found plenty of wild pigs in the bush and wild duck in the nearby streams. Fruit and vegetables, easily grown, became popular foods. Good pasture for their cows ensured a steady supply of the milk, butter and cheese which they particularly enjoyed. The bread and scones which they baked over the fire were made from hand-ground wheat. Within a few years flour mills replaced the hand grinders, and general stores supplemented the home-grown supplies. The first of these was established by D. J. McLeod, still identified by his father's Cape Breton nickname of "Arichat."

So Cape Breton words and ways moved into New Zealand. Along the fern-fringed paths and through the towering forest, men in the tall silk hats and shiny black suits which had come with them from Assynt and St. Ann's strode to church. There Norman ruled still with all the strength and vigour of St. Ann's. Mary, worn by years of ill health, died three years after their coming to Waipu, but Norman seemed untouched by time. In his eighty-first year he frequently rode twelve miles on a Saturday afternoon to one of his churches and preached at nine o'clock that night, then, on Sunday, preached four sermons, two in English and two in Gaelic, and on Monday preached again before returning home to Waipu.

He was now the centre of the community in religious matters only, but this position was enough to ensure his guidance and surveillance of the personal lives of its members. His tenets, firmly inculcated in his people, directed their home life in the smallest detail. "At that time we found our Sunday life at home very hard," wrote one woman, recalling her childhood, "especially when we were not even allowed to go to the clear running brook for a drink of pure water. Enough water to last till Monday had to be brought in on Saturday and it stood in the washtubs which were the only large receptacles available.... Our home used to be a halfway house for cattle drovers. Some of them who did not hold the Sabbath as sacred as our folk, left on the Sabbath day, but my father would not handle their money. Some of them settled on the Saturday night.... We children were always given our Sunday collection money on Saturday night."[1]

All misdemeanours and disputes between members of the settlement were still entirely in Norman's hands. As long as he lived there was no litigation. Instead he conducted an inquiry and disciplined the offenders as he had done in Cape Breton. Fear of a public rebuke from his caustic tongue still constrained the doings of his people.

Although he no longer taught, his influence was strong in the school. The young Edinburgh man, Aeneas Morrison, who became its teacher in 1857, was soon one of his devoted followers. Morrison lived in a small residence attached to the building which served as both church and school. He sometimes read to the people of Waipu when Norman was preaching at Whangarei Heads, and also acted as precentor at the services.

Other schools soon opened and had among their teachers Hugh McKenzie who had taught in Nova Scotia, and Murdoch Fraser, the young diarist of the *Breadalbane*. In New Zealand's thriving economy, the teacher's salary, with a maximum provisionally set at seventy-five pounds a year, was not especially attractive. To procure a teacher for the children in his district John Munro had to reinforce his diplomatic skill with forceful press-gang methods. "The Diplomatist" knew how to pick his men, and the young bank clerk whom he kidnapped from Auckland served long and well as the teacher at Whangarei Heads.

[1] Mrs. Norman Finlayson, quoted in McKenzie, *The Gael Fares Forth*, p. 104.

For this one young man who was drawn into a career in the settlement, there were many within it whom fortune would lure away. In Cape Breton it was usual to be a part-time fisherman, but only a few had sailed far from their own shore until the great adventure of the migration. Now the young generation belonged to the sea. As master mariners they would sail from the great ports of New Zealand to Europe, to the Orient, back to Nova Scotia. They would belong not only to the little Nova Scotian settlements, but, proudly, to the history of New Zealand. Their names—McKenzie, McDonald, Sutherland, Ross, McLeod, Matheson, McGregor, and many more, famous seamen of New Zealand—a roll call of the families who had trusted themselves to the sea on the long voyage from St. Ann's.

In shipbuilding, too, there was honour for the Nova Scotians. To their settlements at Waipu, Whangarei Heads, and Omaha, they quickly transferred the skills of St. Ann's and Baddeck. Trim and graceful, the schooners of Nova Scotian design moved in and out of the New Zealand ports. To the Mathesons of the *Spray* would go prizes for their swift ships—Captain Angus's *Rangatira*, and Captain Duncan's *Three Cheers*, one of the fastest ships that ever sailed in New Zealand waters. In cutters built by McGregors and McMillans, the McKenzies of the *Highland Lass* carried the produce of the Nova Scotian settlements up and down the coast.

On the land and the sea, the community was moving forward in the familiar pattern of its life. Its future would be prosperous. Its strong men were representing it in provincial councils, they were developing its business interests, they were making its name renowned at sea. But in the first days of March, 1866, the strongest of them lay dying, and all other strength was of small account.

The people came to the window of Norman's room. Even in his weakness, they were followed by his admonition and prayers and they understood how deep had been his concern for them. How he, though roughly, had carried them all on his shoulders, how he had felt responsible to God for every single one. Perhaps he had been arrogant in assuming the responsibility, but who can trace the boundary between a strong man's ambition and his duty? For nearly fifty years he had given to his people all the strength of his mind and body and spirit. Although he had never feared for himself he had feared greatly for them. He felt that he had been set, under God, as their defence against the world.

Bitterness against a world he could not trust, the anguish of a father leaving his unprotected family—all his fears for them were in his last words, "Children, children, look to yourselves, the world is mad."

A closely-knit community suffers to accommodate its strong men. As their impulses, their aims, their ideals are greater than the others, so they batter against the confining limits of ordinary life. Made for wider worlds, they find, when they must be contained within a small community, only a few whose strength can answer theirs. From the others the response is either devotion or resentment.

So, through all his life, Norman had challenged his community. He had aroused adoration and bitter hatred. No one could be indifferent to him. As the four bearers carried his coffin on their shoulders along the road to the cemetery, a man who had been unfriendly to Norman stepped up to relieve one of the bearers. The bearer turned on the volunteer, his eyes blazing: "Do you think I would let *you* touch his coffin?" "All right," shrugged the other, turning away, "you can take him to hell yourself."

Before his death, Norman had requested that his people remain united under Aeneas Morrison, the schoolmaster, until the Presbytery appointed his successor. Now they removed his pulpit from the church as a sign that no one was worthy to fill his place. For nearly six years Morrison officiated as lay reader for the congregation, and, even after the induction of an ordained minister he continued to keep as his own following a body of Norman's most devoted admirers. After Morrison's death divisions still persisted in the congregation, and the people remembered how, under Norman's strong hand, individuals had been alienated but segments had never broken off. The antagonisms had all pounded against him, his strength had endured them, and the unity remained.

There would never again be anyone who would take his place at the heart of the community. The ties of blood and kinship would remain, the shared traditions of Assynt and St. Ann's would live for many generations, but with Norman's death the barriers had come down. Now his people belonged to the World.

Further Reading

Archibald, Mrs. Charles. "Early Scottish Settlers in Cape Breton," in *Collections of the Nova Scotia Historical Society*, v. 18, pp. 69-100.

Cape Breton Land Papers. In the Public Archives of Nova Scotia.

Cape Breton School Papers. In the Public Archives of Nova Scotia.

Cape Breton Newspapers Prior to 1855. Microfilm in the Public Archives of Nova Scotia.

Clark, A. J. "The Scottish-Canadian Pilgrims of the Fifties," in Ontario Historical Society *Papers and Records*, v. 26, pp. 5-15.

Dunn, Charles W. *Highland Settler; a Portrait of the Scottish Gael in Nova Scotia.* University of Toronto Press, 1953; reprinted as *Highland Settler: A Portrait of the Scottish Gael in Cape Breton and Eastern Nova Scotia.* Wreck Cove, N.S., Breton Books, 1991.

Grant, Sir Alexander. *The Story of the University of Edinburgh During its First Three Hundred Years*. London, Longmans, 1884.

Haliburton, Thomas Chandler. *An Historical and Statistical Account of Nova Scotia*. Halifax, Joseph Howe, 1829.

Harvey, D. C. "Educational Activities in Cape Breton, 1758-1850," in *Journal of Education*, being the supplement to the report of the Superintendent of Education for Nova Scotia, 4th series, v. 6, September 1935, pp. 518-32.

Harvey, D. C. "Educational Experiments, 1825-32," in *Journal of Education*, 4th series, v. 6, January 1935, pp. 22-29.

Harvey, D. C. "English Schools of Nova Scotia, 1811-25," in *Journal of Education*, 4th series, v. 5, May 1934, pp. 468-79.

Harvey, D. C., ed. *Letters of the Rev. Norman McLeod, 1835-51*. Bulletin of the Public Archives of Nova Scotia, v. 2, no. 1. Halifax, N.S., 1939.

Harvey, D. C. "Origin of our Normal School," in *Journal of Education*, 4th series, v. 8, September 1937, pp. 566-73.

Harvey, D. C. "Struggling Toward an Educational System," in *Journal of Education*, 4th series, v. 6, March 1935, pp. 122-9.

Henderson, John. *General View of the Agriculture of the County of Suther-*

land with Observations on the Means of its Improvement. London, B. McMillan, 1812.

Kennedy, John. *The Days of the Fathers in Ross-shire*. Edinburgh, John Maclaren, 1861.

Lamb, James B. *The Hidden Heritage: Buried Romance at St. Ann's, Nova Scotia*. Windsor, N.S, Lancelot Press, 1975.

Macdonald, Gordon. *The Highlanders of Waipu, or Echoes of 1745*. Dunedin, N.Z., Coulls Somerville Wilkie Ltd., 1928.

McKenzie, N. R. *The Gael Fares Forth; the romantic story of Waipu and Sister Settlements*. Christchurch, N.Z., Whitcombe & Tombs, 1935.

McLeod, Norman. *The Present Church of Scotland and a Tint of Normanism Contending in a Dialogue*. Halifax, N.S., 1843.

Marshall, John G. *Personal Narratives*; with reflections and remarks. Halifax, T. Chamberlain, 1866.

Morgan, Robert J. "'Poverty, wretchedness, and misery': The Great Famine in Cape Breton, 1845-1851," in *Nova Scotia Historical Review*, v. 6, no. 1, 1986.

Morrison, Murdoch. "Migration of Scotch Settlers from St. Ann's, Nova Scotia to New Zealand, 1851-1860," in *Collections of the Nova Scotia Historical Society*, v. 22, pp. 69-95.

Murray, John. *The History of the Presbyterian Church in Cape Breton*. Truro, N.S., 1921.

Patterson, George. *History of the County of Pictou, N.S.* Montreal, Dawson, 1877.

Patterson, George. *Memoir of the Rev. James McGregor, D.D.* Philadelphia, 1859.

Patterson, George, ed. *Remains of Rev. James McGregor*. Philadelphia, Wilson, 1859.

Patterson, George G. *Patterson's History of Victoria County*, with related papers compiled and edited by W. James MacDonald. Sydney, N.S., University College of Cape Breton Press, 1978.

Patterson, George G. *More Studies in Nova Scotian History*. Halifax, N.S., 1941.

Patterson, George G. Notebooks (in Public Archives of Nova Scotia).

Robinson, Neil. *Lion of Scotland*. London, Hodder & Stoughton, 1952.

Sinclair, Sir John. *Statistical Account of Scotland*. Drawn up from the communications of the ministers of the different parishes. Edinburgh, W. Creech, 1791-99.

Stanley, Laurie. *The Well-Watered Garden: The Presbyterian Church in Cape Breton, 1798-1860*. Sydney, N.S., University College of Cape Breton Press, 1983.

Toward, Lilias M. "Influence of Scottish Clergy on Early Education in Cape Breton," in *Collections of the Nova Scotia Historical Society*, v. 29, pp. 153-77.

Uniacke, Richard John. *Uniacke's Sketches of Cape Breton and Other Papers Relating to Cape Breton Island*, ed. with an introduction and notes by C. Bruce Fergusson. Halifax, Public Archives of Nova Scotia, 1958.

Wilson, Robert. *Historical Account and Delineation of Aberdeen*. Aberdeen, J. Johnston, 1822.

ALSO AVAILABLE FROM Breton Books

■ **THE MOONLIGHT SKATER** by Beatrice MacNeil
9 Cape Breton Stories & The Dream
A mischievous blend of Scottish & Acadian, these stories blossom, or explode softly, in your life. Plus her classic play set in rural Cape Breton.
$9.00

■ **ECHOES FROM LABOR'S WARS** by Dawn Fraser
Industrial Cape Breton in the 1920s • Echoes of World War One
Autobiography & Other Writings
Dawn Fraser's narrative verse and stories are a powerful, compelling testament to courage, peace & community. They belong in every home, in every school.
$11.25

■ **CAPE BRETON CAPTAIN** by Captain David A. McLeod
Reminiscences from 50 Years Afloat and Ashore
A rough-and-tumble autobiography of sailing, shipwreck, mutiny, and love.
$14.25

■ **ARCHIE NEIL** by Mary Anne Ducharme
From the Life & Stories of Archie Neil Chisholm of Margaree Forks, C. B.
Mary Anne Ducharme's extraordinary book melds oral history, biography and an anthology of stories into "the triumph of a life."
$16.75

■ **CASTAWAY ON CAPE BRETON**
Two Great Shipwreck Narratives in One Book
1. Ensign Prenties' *Narrative* of Shipwreck at Margaree Harbour, 1780
Edited with an Historical Setting and Notes by G. G. Campbell
2. Samuel Burrows' *Narrative* of Shipwreck on the Cheticamp Coast, 1823
With Notes on Acadians Who Cared for the Survivors by Charles D. Roach
$11.25

■ **DOWN NORTH: The Original Book of Cape Breton's Magazine**
Word-and-Photo Portrait of Cape Breton • 239 pages, 286 photographs
$22.35

■ **CAPE BRETON LIVES: A Second Book from Cape Breton's Magazine**
300 pages of Life Stories • 120 photographs
$22.35

■ **HIGHLAND SETTLER** by Charles W. Dunn
A Portrait of the Scottish Gael in Cape Breton and Eastern Nova Scotia
"This is one of the best books yet written on the culture of the Gaels of Cape Breton and one of the few good studies of a folk-culture." *Western Folklore*
$14.25

CONTINUED NEXT PAGE